Jump into Science

Additional Gryphon House Books Written by Rae Pica:

Great Games
Jump into Literacy
Jump into Math
Teachable Transitions
Wiggle, Giggle, & Shake

The Learning in Leaps and Bounds Series

Jump into SCIENCE

Active Learning for Preschool Children

Rae Pica

Illustrated by
Kathi Whelan Dery

Gryphon House, Inc.
Beltsville, MD

Jump into
Science

© 2009 Rae Pica
Published by Gryphon House, Inc.
PO Box 207, Beltsville, MD 20704
800.638.0928; 301.595.9500; 301.595.0051 (fax)

Visit us on the web at www.gryphonhouse.com

Illustrations: Kathi Whelan Dery

Library of Congress Cataloging-in-Publication Data

Pica, Rae, 1953-
  Jump into science : active learning for preschool children / by Rae Pica.
       p. cm.
  Includes bibliographical references and index.
  ISBN 978-0-87659-056-0
  1. Science--Study and teaching (Early childhood) 2. Early childhood
education--Activity programs. I. Title.
  LB1139.5.S35P53 2009
  372.35'044--dc22

                    2008040912

Bulk purchase

Gryphon House books are available for special premiums and sales promotions as well as for
fund-raising use. Special editions or book excerpts also can be created to specification. For
details, contact the Director of Marketing at Gryphon House.

Disclaimer

Gryphon House, Inc. and the author cannot be held responsible for damage, mishap, or
injury incurred during the use of or because of activities in this book. Appropriate and
reasonable caution and adult supervision of children involved in activities and corresponding
to the age and capability of each child involved, is recommended at all times. Do not leave
children unattended at any time. Observe safety and caution at all times.

Gryphon House is a member of the Green Press Initiative, a nonprofit
program dedicated to supporting publishers in their efforts to reduce their
use of fiber-sourced forests. This book is made of 30% post-consumer
waste. For further information visit www.greenpressinitiative.org.

Table of Contents

Introduction

As a movement specialist for nearly 30 years, I've seen the response to my topic wax and wane. At first, no one wanted to hear that children should be more active because they imagined the chaos that would result. Watching early childhood professionals recoil at my suggestion that children learn with their whole bodies, I felt the way a dentist must when approaching a patient with drill in hand!

Gradually, the early childhood field accepted the reality that children are active learners. Teachers realized that children were going to be active regardless. They could either fight children's need for movement or use it. (It was the educational equivalent of "If you can't beat 'em, join 'em.")

Today I find that most early childhood professionals are fully aware of the many benefits of physical activity and play, including how they contribute to the cognitive domain. They understand that young children are experiential learners, and that the more senses used in the learning process, the more children retain (Fauth, 1990). Moreover, Gardner's (1993) recognition of the bodily/kinesthetic intelligence has validated the use of the body and parts of the body as a way of learning and knowing. Brain research also confirms that the mind and body are not separate entities—that the functions of the body contribute to the functions of the mind (Hannaford, 2005; Jensen, 2000).

However, with the clamor for more accountability and testing, seatwork is once again threatening to supplant active learning. Even physical education and recess are being eliminated in favor of more "academic time" (ironically, in an age when there's never been greater concern about childhood obesity). As a result, teachers are feeling pressured to teach young children in ways they know are developmentally inappropriate.

But children haven't changed. To understand concepts fully, children still need to explore the meaning of concepts with their bodies, and that includes science concepts. Teachers, having accepted that children are active learners, are frustrated at being asked to "teach" science with drills and worksheets.

Science in Early Childhood

The word *science* may bring to mind men and women in lab coats, working with beakers, burners, and microscopes. It may prompt memories of concepts learned in chemistry, physics, or biology classes, or bring to mind such topics as botany or astronomy. But that clearly is an adult perception of science. And if that's your only perception of science, you might wonder—rightly—what place the subject has in the early childhood curriculum.

Science for young children, however, is not about concoctions in test tubes. It doesn't involve technical terms and scientific formulas. Rather, because science is about exploration, discovery, investigation, and problem solving, it can be said that every young child is a scientist—because their early lives are all about exploring and investigating the world around them! Everything children encounter is a mystery or a problem to be solved—a discovery waiting to be made.

More specifically, children first discover the workings of their own bodies. There are different ways to move—first while remaining in one place and eventually while traveling through the surrounding space. There are body parts to be discovered. Where are they, and what do they do? What are they called? Children learn that their bodies are something that must be cared for through good nutrition and hygiene. Thus, the "study" of the human body, which falls under the heading of health science, is one of the themes commonly explored in early childhood classrooms, and is the starting point for the activities in this book.

As children become increasingly aware of the world around them, they encounter animals, birds, and bugs in their own homes, outdoors, and, perhaps, through such venues as zoos and their preschool classroom. While zoology and other animal sciences are beyond their scope, young children are anxious to learn more about how these creatures move, the sounds they make, and how they are alike and different. Because young children are fascinated by creatures that are not other people, the theme of animals is one of the most popular in the early childhood curriculum. This theme is part of life science.

Of course, as young children mature and are exposed to life beyond the insides of their homes, they become aware of the elements of weather and seasonal changes. They're intrigued by rain, snow, wind, and the discovery of shadows, seeds, and falling leaves. Plants and animals are part of life science, while the elements of weather are components of Earth and space science.

Finally, there are simple scientific concepts which young children can and should explore: flotation, electricity, gravity, balance, sound, air, evaporation and absorption, magnetism, and machinery (all falling under physical science). Naturally, it's inappropriate to try to explain how electricity works or to define the force of gravity. You may never even use such words as *gravity* and *evaporation* with the children, but that doesn't mean they can't be introduced to the concepts through simple, developmentally appropriate experiences.

Science process skills are categorized as basic, intermediate, and advanced. Preschoolers can—and should—experience the basic process skills: observing, comparing, classifying, measuring, and communicating (Charlesworth & Lind, 2003). Behind these skills and most important to science learning, according to

Charlesworth and Lind, is *curiosity*. They contend that curiosity is one of the most important attitudes anyone can have because curiosity inspires new perspectives and questions, which are essential to scientific exploration. They write: "This approach that is basic to science is natural to young children. They use all their senses and energies to find out about the world around them" (p.65).

The Rationale for Active Learning in Science

Because young children are concrete thinkers and experiential learners, they need to explore science concepts with appropriate activities. For instance, gravity is the concept involved when children jump into the air and return to the ground. Evaporation is what occurs when children "paint" an outside wall with water and the water gradually disappears. Although young children may not understand how these things work, they can witness and feel them. Young children acquire so much information through their senses; the more senses involved in their learning process, the more children learn.

For too long, people have believed that the mind and body are separate entities and that the functions of the mind are superior to the functions of the body. That belief led to the popular notion that children must sit still in school in order to learn. Unfortunately, although early childhood education was once the exception to this mandate, even preschoolers are now being asked to do increasingly more seatwork and paperwork.

Research, in particular the latest brain research, has demonstrated that the mind and body are not separate entities. In fact, the functions of the body make a considerable contribution to the functions of the mind. For example, lessons that are physically experienced have a more immediate and longer-lasting impact. In addition, integrating body systems enables optimal learning to occur (Jensen, 2000). Studies have also shown that more of the brain is activated during physical activity than while doing seatwork (Jensen, 2000). But perhaps the most important fact for us to know is that young children prefer to learn through movement!

Of course, it's easy to imagine that children learn more from time spent with computer programs, or being drilled with flashcards and test questions. They can recognize letters or shapes, recite their ABCs, and count to 50. But this and similar feats represent rote learning—the result of sheer memorization. Authentic learning involves comprehension. And until the information has some relevance to the child's life, there'll be no comprehension.

Rote learning has its place, of course; it's how most of us learned the multiplication tables and the state capitals. However, unless a child is going to grow up to become a contestant on television game shows, memorizing facts will have little use in life once she's passed all the tests school requires of her. Authentic learning, on the other hand—the process of exploration and discovery, of acquiring knowledge, of knowing how to acquire it (no one can memorize all the facts!) —will serve her endlessly. Moreover, active and authentic learning is far more likely than rote learning to foster a lifelong love of the learning process.

Consider the difference between a child being told about flotation versus his investigation and imitation of bubbles drifting in the air. Between his being told about balance versus figuring out for himself what happens when he leans just far enough in a certain direction. Being told that cats move quietly and turtles move slowly versus experiencing those kinds of movement himself.

Jensen (2001) labels this kind of active learning implicit—like learning to ride a bike. At the opposite end of the spectrum is explicit learning—like being told the capital of Peru. He asks, "If you hadn't ridden a bicycle for five years, could you still do it? But if you hadn't heard the name of the capital of Peru for five years, would you still know it?" (p.74). (Indeed, how many of us can still recite the definitions of gravity or absorption, or explain how electricity is conducted?)

Extrinsic learning may be quicker than learning through physical experiences, but the latter has greater meaning for children and stays with them longer. There are many reasons for this, including the fact that intrinsic learning creates more neural networks in the brain and employs more senses. Another reason may be that it's simply more fun! As music educator Jaques-Dalcroze (1931) said: "I look upon joy as the most powerful of all mental stimuli."

What Science, Movement, & Music Have in Common

Teachers in preschool and through the early elementary grades tell me that they often don't have time anymore to include movement and music in the curriculum. There are standards to be met and tests to be taken—primarily in the area of literacy—and movement and music are increasingly viewed as "frills" by administrators and parents. Both teachers and children lament the loss of two of the most popular subjects in their classrooms.

But they don't have to lose movement and music! Of course, it may no longer be acceptable to run, jump, and sing just for the joy—and the physical and social/emotional benefits—of it. But what if movement and music have *cognitive* benefits? What if they can be used to help children meet those standards and pass those tests? What if the notion that movement/music and science are mutually exclusive is simply incorrect?

The fact is, movement and music are essential to active learning; and movement, music, and science are easily linked. For example, as mentioned, science for young children begins with the body; and what children's bodies are most known for is moving. How much better is it for children to learn to recognize and use body parts by employing them in a variety of physical activities? How much better is it for children to consider the functions of their heart, lungs, and muscles by stimulating them through movement? How much better is it for children to experience the sense of hearing by actively listening to a piece of music and discovering that just as a piece of music has a rhythm, so too do our hearts and breathing?

Moreover, when children physically experience concepts, they are learning through exploration and discovery. And, as pointed out earlier, exploration and discovery are what science is all about. Both science and movement involve learning by doing.

How to Use This Book

The activities I've chosen for *Jump into Science* offer children opportunities to physically and fully experience — through their bodies and/or their voices— concepts falling under the headings of the human body; the five senses; animals and other creatures; the seasons, weather, and other natural wonders; and simple science. These components make up the main sections of this book.

Every activity in the book begins with information about how the activity supports science learning as well as information to share with the children before starting. Next, the heading "To Have" lists any materials or advance preparation that is needed (most activities require no materials). "To Do" explains how to teach the activity. If an activity has extensions, they are listed under the heading "More to Do." When relevant children's literature or music is available, it is included along with an identifying icon—a book for literature and a musical note for recordings—to make them easy to identify. Use these suggested books and recordings to extend the children's learning.

The chapters of the book appear in developmental order, from least to most challenging. To the best of my ability, I've also placed the activities within each section according to its level of difficulty.

Still, it isn't possible to use the activities, one after the other, in the order in which they appear in the book. The reason is that they don't progress in a neat, step-by-step sequence, from point A to point Z, nor do children learn in that manner. There's a lot of interrelatedness among these scientific areas, and children acquire knowledge in overlapping ways.

My suggestion is that you begin with the simplest activities under The Human Body, repeating them as long as the children remain interested. (It's likely you'll tire of them long before the children do, but that's okay; repetition is essential to reinforcing learning in early childhood!) Skip—and mark—those extensions that are currently too challenging for the children. Then move on to the simplest activities under The Five Senses. Continue in this manner, letting the children alert you to when it's time to move on. (They should be experiencing at least an 80% success rate. When activities are too simple for them, they'll become bored. When activities are too difficult for them, the children will become frustrated.)

When you've completed all the activities the children are capable of doing in each of the chapters, return to The Human Body. Repeat any activities you feel need reinforcing. For those with extensions, you should repeat the initial activity and then try the extension. Again, when you reach a point where the children are no longer experiencing more success than failure, move on to The Five Senses, repeating and extending as you see fit.

Whether you use these activities during circle or group time, substitute them for more "traditional" lessons in science, or use them as follow-ups to traditional lessons, you can be sure the children are moving in leaps and bounds toward becoming capable scientists. Moreover, because you will have taught to the *whole child*—employing the physical and social/emotional, as well as the cognitive—you can be sure the lessons learned here will be long-lasting and meaningful.

CHAPTER 1

The Human Body

"Study" of the human body, which falls under the category of health science, is where science starts for young children. As infants, they begin to discover the parts of their bodies and as toddlers can identify at least six of the parts of their bodies. By the time children are seven, they know where and what most of their body parts are. Still, many a child has arrived in the early and even upper-elementary grades not knowing his elbow from his shoulder. This chapter, therefore, offers many body-part identification activities, including such old favorites as "Where Is Thumbkin?"

Of course, even when children know the "what" and "where" of the parts of their bodies, it doesn't mean they fully understand how to use them. As children take part in the activities involving various body parts, they're given the opportunity to discover their capabilities and limitations.

Then there are such "hidden" body parts as the heart, muscles, and lungs. This chapter has activities that also call children's attention to the functions of these health-related parts of the human body, serving as an introduction to fitness.

Finally, the concepts of *hygiene* and *nutrition* are addressed in this chapter, too, helping children consider the need to take good care of their bodies, while making it all enjoyable!

Promotes observation skills and anatomical awareness

Where Is Thumbkin?

In this old favorite, children learn whimsical names for each of their fingers. This activity promotes awareness of basic anatomy, and it reinforces the science skills of observation and comparison. Because the children perform the song and fingerplay, they also gain enrichment in the areas of music and language arts.

To Have

No materials needed

To Do

- Begin by having the children look at their own fingers. Ask them to compare their fingers. Which is the longest? Which is the shortest? Which is the fattest? Next, have the children compare their own fingers to a friend's. You may point out that, for some people, the middle finger is the longest. For others, the ring finger is longer than the middle finger. Talk about the names for each finger.
- Sing the song below, asking the whereabouts of thumbkin, pointer, middle finger, ring finger, pinkie, and the whole family. Hide your fingers behind your back until the children sing the response "Here I am" for each finger.
- When you sing the question "How are you this morning?" have the children respond, "Very well, I thank you." Show them how to have the finger on one hand ask the question while the corresponding finger on the other hand responds.

Where Is Thumbkin? (Traditional)

Where is thumbkin,	*How are you this morning?*
Where is thumbkin?	*Very well, I thank you,*
Here I am, here I am.	*Run and hide, run and hide.*

(additional verses)

Where is pointer…	*Where is pinkie…*
Where is middle finger…	*Where's the whole family…*
Where is ring finger…	

You will find this fingerplay in *The Eentsy, Weentsy Spider: Fingerplays and Action Rhymes* by Joanna Cole, Stephanie Calmenson, and Alan Tiegreen.

Children will enjoy listening to the CD *Where Is Thumbkin?*, which is designed to accompany Pam Schiller and Thomas Moore's book of the same name.

Counting Fingers

This simple activity calls attention to the muscles that allow us to move our fingers and hands. Opening and closing one finger at a time can be a difficult task for young children. It may take several repetitions for them to get the hang of it, but repetition will help reinforce counting and sequencing skills. As an added bonus, this activity improves fine-motor coordination.

To Have

No materials needed

To Do

- Invite the children to curl their hands into loose fists.
- As you count slowly from one to ten, have the children open one finger at a time.
- Now count from ten to one, having the children curl each finger, one at a time, back into the palm of their hands.
- When the children tire of this activity, ask them to think of some animals they know. How many fingers or toes do they have? What is the difference between fingers and toes? You might tell the children that some animals, such as deer, have only two toes on each hoof. Rabbits have four toes on each paw. Raccoons have five "fingers" on each "hand."

More to Do

- Challenge the children to wiggle their fingers without moving their hands!
- Encourage the children to pretend they are playing a piano.

Madcap monkeys explain hands, fingers, and thumbs to beginning readers in *Hand, Hand, Fingers, Thumb* by Al Perkins. Children will also enjoy *The Kissing Hand* by Audrey Penn, which is a charming tale about a baby raccoon that gets a kiss on the hand from his mother before going off to school.

Try counting fingers to music with "I Have Ten Little Fingers," from *Fingerplays and Footplays* by Rosemary Hallum and Henry Buzz Glass or "I Can Count to Ten" on *Playing and Learning with Music* by Maryann "Mar" Harman.

The Human Body

Develops the concept of muscles and promotes observation skills

Open & Close

This activity creates awareness of muscles and how they move different parts of the body. It begins with the hands and moves on to identifying other body parts. Because children learn to use such opposite verbs as open *and* close, *the activity also promotes emergent literacy.*

To Have

No materials needed

To Do

- Lead the children in opening and closing their hands, at varying tempos. Have them stretch their fingers to their limit (comfortably) and then clench their fists very tightly.
- As the children do this, use the words *open* and *close* to reinforce these opposite verbs.
- Ask the children if they can feel the muscles moving their hands. Explain that there are muscles in other parts of the body, too. Tell the children that they can find out where some of these muscles are by discovering other body parts that open and close. Some of these include eyes, mouth, arms, and legs.

More to Do

- Invite the children to curl up on the floor (a "closed" position) and then slowly stretch out their whole body (an "open" position). Then have the children reverse the process.

Closed

Open

The Mirror Game

This activity introduces the science concept of reflection, and it promotes the use of simple tools, such as mirrors, for observation. As an added bonus, children learn to replicate physically what they see.

To Have

Full-size unbreakable mirror (optional)

To Do

- Begin by talking with the children about mirrors. Where have you noticed mirrors? What are some of the uses of mirrors? For example, you might talk about mirrors to look into as you brush your teeth, rear-view mirrors used in cars, or mirrors that the dentist uses to see into the corners of your mouth.
- Stand and face the children so that they all have a clear view of you. Ask the children to imagine that you are looking into a mirror. If you are looking in a mirror, then they must be your reflections. That means they must do exactly what you do.
- Silently perform simple poses or movements. For example, stand briefly on one foot or lift and lower your arms. Move slowly from one position to the next so that the children can copy you.

More to Do

- For a greater challenge, hop or jump in place, wave your arms, or shake different parts of your body.
- Bring in a full-size mirror and encourage the children to take turns moving different body parts in front of it.
- When the children are ready to work cooperatively, have them perform the Mirror Game in partners, taking turns leading and "reflecting."
- Ask the children if they can think of other things that make reflections. Some examples might include the still water of a pond, the shiny back of a spoon, or a store window.

No Mirrors in My Nana's House, written by Ysaye Barnwell, includes a musical CD.

Also try Ella Jenkins' song, "I Looked into the Mirror," from the CD *Jambo and Other Call-and-Response Songs and Chants.*

The Human Body

Introduces the concepts of light and shadow

Shadow Dancing

This activity enhances body awareness while introducing two basic concepts of physical science—light and shadow.

To Have

Large white sheet
Lamp
Recorded music

To Do

- String up the sheet to create a screen.
- Have the children face the screen.
- Set up a lamp so that it is behind the children. When you turn on the lamp, the children's shadows should appear on the screen.
- Turn on the lamp, start the music, and invite the children to move any way they want. Encourage them to describe how their shadows move on the screen.
- Ask the children to experiment with the shadows by moving forward and back. When do the shadows get bigger? When are they smaller?
- Periodically, rotate the children so everyone has a chance to be in front. Also, change the style of the music playing to inspire different kinds of movement!

Play "My Shadow" from the CD *Vincent and the Big Bad Kitchen Band.*

Pairs of Parts

This activity reinforces body awareness and offers experience with numbers. Because it introduces the verb and noun pair, *it also enhances emergent literacy. As an added bonus, this activity gives children the chance to giggle over the absurdity of having three noses or five eyes!*

To Have

No materials needed

To Do

- Explain to the children that there are many parts of the body that come in twos, or *pairs*. Ask the children to list some of these *pairs*, for example, eyes, ears, nostrils, hands, knees, and feet.
- Once the children have had ample time to discover pairs of body parts, invite them to think of other parts that do not come in pairs. Some possibilities include fingers, toes, teeth, and eyelashes.

More to Do

- Encourage the children to think of animals that have body parts that come in pairs. Some examples could include birds with two wings, bugs with two antennae, fish with two fins, and elephants with two big ears.

Roberta Grobel Intrater's board book *Two Eyes, a Nose, and a Mouth* would be a good accompaniment to this activity.

"The Body Poem" from Rae Pica and Richard Gardzina's CD *Wiggle, Giggle, & Shake* is a fun way to consider pairs of body parts.

Wash Your Hands

Washing hands is one of the most important aspects of good hygiene, and it is a fundamental concept in health science. This activity makes the whole concept seem like fun!

To Have

No materials needed

To Do

- Begin by introducing the concept of *germs*. Explain that germs are too small to see, but they can make people sick. Germs are the reason people get colds, sore throats, and other illnesses. Ask the children if they know how they can help get rid of germs.
- Tell the children that they are going to pretend to get rid of germs. Have them stand in a circle, as if they are gathered around a big sink.
- Suggest that the children act out the lyrics below while singing the following song to the tune of "London Bridge":

Soap Our Hands by Rae Pica
This is how we soap our hands,
Soap our hands, soap our hands.
This is how we soap our hands,
So we can get them clean.

This is how we wash our hands,
Wash our hands, wash our hands.
This is how we wash our hands,
So we can get them clean.

This is how we dry our hands,
Dry our hands, dry our hands.
This is how we dry our hands,
And now they're nice and clean.

Read and discuss *Those Mean Nasty Dirty Downright Disgusting but...Invisible Germs* by Judith Anne Rice, or *Wash Up!* by Gwenyth Swain.

Rub-a-dub-dub

Good hygiene is an important concept in health science. Children may not like taking a bath at home, but they will love taking a pretend bath in the classroom!

To Have

Chiffon scarves (1 per child)

To Do

- Talk to the children about bathing.
- Have the children pretend they are sitting in a tub. Give them each a scarf to use as a washcloth. Invite the children to wash each of the following body parts as you call them out:
  - Face
  - Behind the ears
  - Neck
  - Hands
  - Arms
  - Chest
  - Tummy
  - Back
  - Legs
  - Feet
  - Toes

Read *Scrubba Dub* by Nancy Van Laan or *Do Pirates Take Baths?* by Kathy Tucker.

There are plenty of bathing songs to choose from! Hap Palmer's *Learning Basic Skills through Music*, Vol. III includes songs such as "Take a Bath" and "Keep the Germs Away." *Vincent and the Big Bad Kitchen Band* includes "Double Bubble Bath." Carole Peterson's *Tiny Tunes: Music for the Very Young Child* features "The Bathtub Song." Music with Mar's *Playing and Learning with Music* includes "I Like My Bath."

The Human Body 21

Reinforces good hygiene and introduces the concept of mammals

I Love My Hair

All humans are mammals. Having hair is just one of the things that make us mammals. This activity introduces children to the concept of classification and the term mammal. *It also provides an opportunity to talk about the diversity of hair color and styles of the children in the classroom.*

This activity introduces children to this important science concept. Hair care is an important part of hygiene. Before beginning this activity, you might talk to the children about their hair, pointing out the diversity in hair color and styles.

To Have

Pictures of animals with hair
Pictures of animals with feathers or scales
Pictures of people with different hairstyles (optional)

To Do

- Begin by looking at photos of animals with hair. How is their hair the same or different? Ask the children "Do birds have hair?" or "Do lizards or fish have hair?" Explain that not all animals have hair. Those that do have hair are called *mammals*. People are mammals, too!
- Next, talk to the children about their hair. Point out the diversity in hair color and styles. Ask the children why they think people wash their hair.
- Invite the children to pretend to do the following:
  - Shampoo their hair (massaging the scalp and working the shampoo all through their hair)
  - Rinse their hair
  - Towel their hair dry
  - Blow their hair dry
  - Comb or brush their hair!

More to Do

- Invite the children to pretend they are hairstylists and barbers at work.

Read *I Love My Hair!* by Natasha Anastasia Tarpley and E.B. Lewis.

Statues & Rag Dolls

When you ask children to pretend they are statues and rag dolls, you are getting the children to contract and relax their muscles. This will help them to understand how their muscles work, especially if you ask them to think about how tight their muscles are when they are statues, and how loose they are as rag dolls. This activity is a great relaxation exercise to use any time the children need to wind down a bit.

To Have

Pictures or examples of statues and rag dolls (optional)

Recorded music (optional)

To Do

- Talk to the children about statues, or show them pictures of various statues.
- Ask the children to pretend they are statues. Have them use words to describe how they feel.
- Repeat the first two steps, this time with rag dolls.
- When they have the idea, challenge the children to alternate between statue and rag doll. You can call out the words or use some other signal. Vary the time between signals so the children cannot anticipate when your next signal is coming!

More to Do

- Play a game of Statues. Encourage the children to move in any way they want while you play music. Have them freeze like statues whenever you press the pause button. Be sure to vary the length of time between each change.

Greg & Steve's *Kids in Motion* includes a song called "The Freeze." You may also try these Hap Palmer recordings: "Rock and Roll Freeze Dance" from *So Big* and "Rag Doll" from *Pretend*.

The Human Body

Feeling Fit

When children take part in physical activity of moderate to vigorous intensity, it increases the heart rate, promotes cardiovascular endurance, and helps develop strong bones, muscles, and joints.

To Have

Recorded music with a lively tempo

To Do

- Talk with the children about the importance of physical activity.
- Next, play a Follow-the-Leader game in which you lead the children around the room at moderate to vigorous levels of intensity. Appropriate movements include walking quickly, jogging, marching, or galloping.
- Gradually slow your movement toward the end, giving the children a chance to cool down.

More to Do

- Put on a recorded march and invite the children to pretend they are in a parade. Encourage them to lift their knees and swing their arms!
- Play a piece of lively music and invite the children to move to it in any way they want. (Asking children to "dance" can be too intimidating for some children.)

Read *My Amazing Body: A First Look at Health and Fitness* by Pat Thomas. You may also try Lizzy Rockwell's *The Busy Body Book: A Kid's Guide to Fitness.*

Hap Palmer's *Mod Marches* includes good songs for marching. *Aerobic Dances for Kids* by Henry Buzz Glass and Rosemary Hallum has lively music for dancing and movement activities.

Energy In/Energy Out

Energy in/energy out is the formula referring to the number of calories consumed/burned. When the number of calories consumed exceeds the number of calories burned, weight gain is inevitable. When the number is in balance, individuals are able to maintain their weight and thus their health. A balance in appropriate foods is another way to stay healthy.

To Have

Plastic hoops in five different colors
Lively music

To Do

- Space the hoops throughout the room and explain that each color represents a food group: vegetables, fruits, dairy products, whole grains, and proteins.
- When the music starts, the children should accompany it with energetic movement (energy out).
- When the music stops, the children run to one of the "food groups," where they pretend to eat.
- Repeat this process several times, encouraging the children to make sure to visit all four food groups throughout the game.

The Human Body

Promotes awareness of how hands can communicate

Hands in Action

This activity offers an opportunity for the children to consider all the things their hands "say." It also helps to reinforce word comprehension.

To Have

No materials needed

To Do

- Talk to the children about how people communicate. People write, and they can even "say" things with their hands.
- Invite the children to sit and show you, with their hands alone, the following actions. Discuss the meaning of these words and use them in sentences to help with comprehension:

  - Clap
  - Pat
  - Tap
  - Wring

  - Sew
  - Stroke
  - Wave
  - Beckon

  - Pinch
  - Pluck
  - Strum
  - Fan

More to Do

- Ask the children to show you how they can "say" the following words using only their hands:

  - "Hello."
  - "Come here."
  - "Go away."

  - "I'm scared."
  - "I'm cold."
  - "I'm worried."

  - "I'm hot."
  - "I'm hungry."
  - "Goodbye."

Hands Are Not for Hitting by Martine Agassi explores other uses for hands such as waving, drawing, and making music.

Ambrose Brazelton's *Clap, Snap, and Tap* and Jill Gallina's *Hand-Jivin'* offer plenty of rhythmic hand movements. The song "Hands," from *Songs for Peacemakers* by Max and Marcia Nass, teaches that "hands are for loving…not pushing and shoving."

I Love My Clothes

Caring for clothing is as much a part of good hygiene as caring for the body. This activity gives children the opportunity to consider the effort that should go into taking good care of the clothes they put on their body.

To Have

No materials needed

To Do

- Invite the children to demonstrate the actions involved in doing the following:
  - Putting clothes into the washing machine
  - Hanging clothes on a clothesline
  - Taking clothes out of the dryer
  - Washing an item of clothing by hand
  - Ironing
  - Folding clothes
  - Putting clothes on hangers

Book possibilities include *My Clothes / Mi Ropa* by Rebecca Emberley, *Get Dressed* by Gwenyth Swain, and *All Kinds of Clothes* by Jeri S. Cipriano.

Deep Breathing

This activity focuses the children's attention on the breathing process. Because it involves deep breathing, it also promotes relaxation. This is a good activity to use any time the children need to wind down.

To Have

Balloon

To Do

- Demonstrate inflation and deflation by blowing up a balloon then letting the air out of it.
- Explain that our lungs do the same thing as the balloon. They inflate and deflate as we breathe in and out. Point out that our lungs inflate and deflate slowly.
- Ask the children to imagine that each of them is a balloon. Tell them they can be whatever color they want to be.
- Have the children pretend to "inflate" by inhaling slowly through the nose and then "deflate" by exhaling slowly through the mouth. Repeat this activity a couple of times until the children have achieved a level of relaxation. Be sure that they do not do this so often that they hyperventilate!

More to Do

- Ask the children to pretend to be balloons floating in the sky. Point out that their muscles are relaxed when they are pretending to float.

Read *Emily's Balloon* by Komako Sakai or *I Spy a Balloon* by Jean Marzollo.

Let It Blow

This activity introduces the concept of air resistance. Since the children are providing the air with their own lungs, this activity also reinforces their understanding of how their bodies work. Additionally, it encourages cooperation.

To Have

Parachute

A feather

Cotton balls (optional)

To Do

- The children sit in a circle around the parachute and lift it to chin level. Place a feather in the center of the parachute, and invite the children to work together to blow it off!

More to Do

- Put a cotton ball on the parachute and challenge the children to discover whether it is easier or harder to blow it off than the feather was.
- Place three different objects of increasing weights on the parachute, one after the other. Ask the children to try to blow each. Which is the easiest to move? Which is the hardest to move?

Share the book *Feathers for Lunch!* by Lois Ehlert.

Introduces the concept of food as energy and promotes nutrition

Peanut Butter & Jelly

This activity is a fun way to introduce different food groups. Explain to the children that peanut butter is made from crushed peanuts. These contain a lot of protein. People need to eat protein to build muscles. Jelly is made from different fruits, which are carbohydrates. Carbohydrates are used for energy to make our bodies go.

To Have

No materials needed

To Do

- Talk to the children about where their bodies get energy. Explain that energy comes from the foods they eat. Peanut butter and jelly sandwiches are just one way to get energy. Ask how many children like peanut butter and jelly.
- Whisper the words "jelly" or "peanut butter" into the ear of each child. Then, give the children a signal to start walking round the room. When a child comes face to face with another player, both children say the word you said to them. If one says "jelly" and the other "peanut butter," the children hug to make a "peanut butter and jelly sandwich." Then, they continue around the room. If both children say the same word, they just move along. The goal is for the children to make as many "peanut butter and jelly sandwiches" as possible before you give the signal to stop.

More to Do

- Substitute *bread* and *butter* for the words *peanut butter* and *jelly*. Explain that bread is made from grains such as wheat. Bread is also a carbohydrate. Butter is a kind of fat made from milk. (*Salt* and *pepper* or *ketchup* and *mustard* are also good combinations to try.)
- You may also try this game having the children shake hands when they come face to face.

Share the book *From Peanut to Peanut Butter* by Robin Nelson.

You can play the song "Peanut Butter" from *Fingerplays and Footplays* by Rosemary Hallum and Henry "Buzz" Glass. Also, try "Peanut Butter and Jelly" from *Fun and Games* by Greg & Steve. *Late Last Night* by Joe Scruggs has the songs "Peanut Butter and Jelly" and "Grape Jelly Cure."

Heart to Heart

In the past, children spent much of their free time running and jumping and getting their heart rates up. Giving the heart regular exercise is critical to good health. Unfortunately, children today lead more sedentary lives. They are not getting their heart rates up often enough. This activity introduces the heart as part of the cardiovascular system and discusses the importance of keeping it healthy.

To Have

No materials needed

To Do

- Sit on the floor or ground with the children and show them how they can feel their heartbeat either by placing a hand on their chest or their fingers on their throat. After they locate their heartbeat, give them a few moments to get a sense of its rhythm and pace. You may explain that the reason they can feel their heartbeat in their throat is because their hearts are pumping blood through their bodies.

- Invite the children to run in place as fast as they can (or, if you have enough space, the children can run around freely). After about a minute, give them a signal to stop and sit. Once again, they should locate their heartbeat. Is it going faster now?

- Explain that it is a good thing for their heart to beat faster after exercise. The heart is a muscle that needs exercise to stay healthy!

Everybody Dance is a CD filled with heart-pumping tempos.

The Human Body   31

Promotes awareness of nutrition and teaches where vegetables come from

Eat Your Veggies

Although vegetables are the most important food group, they are not typically popular with young children. Perhaps once the children work with vegetables and pretend to be vegetables, they will look at them with more appreciation!

To Have

Pictures of various vegetables

To Do

- Talk to the children about the vegetables in this activity, showing them pictures of different vegetables. You can explain that some vegetables, such as zucchini, are containers that carry seeds for a plant to grow. Carrots are roots that grow underground. Lettuce is made of leaves and broccoli is made of flower buds.
- One at a time, ask the children to take on the shape of these vegetables:

- Carrot
- Potato
- Zucchini or yellow squash
- A head of lettuce

- Onion
- Pea
- Green bean
- Broccoli stalk

More to Do

- Invite the children to pretend they are doing the following veggie-related activities:

- Pulling a carrot out of the ground
- Scraping a carrot
- Washing lettuce
- Pulling apart lettuce leaves

- Chopping an onion
- Peeling a potato
- Mashing potatoes
- Scooping up a forkful of peas

Share the following books with the children: Grace Lin's *The Ugly Vegetables*, Lois Ehlert's *Growing Vegetable Soup*, Hannah Tofts' *I Eat Vegetables!* and Jerry Pallotta's *The Vegetable Alphabet Book*.

Cathy Slonecki's *Nutricise* includes "The Vegetable Rock," and Laurie Berkner's *Buzz Buzz* includes "The Valley of Vegetables."

Tooty-Fruity

Like the last activity, this one has children pretending to be food—this time in the form of fruit.

To Have

Pictures of various fruits

To Do

- Talk to the children about the fruit mentioned below. Show the children pictures of the different fruits. Discuss how some fruits, like oranges, have seeds inside for plants to grow. Point out how strawberries have seeds on the outside.
- Invite the children to take on the shape of the following fruits:
  - Orange
  - Banana
  - Pumpkin
  - Blueberry
  - Lemon
  - Pear

More to Do

- Introduce the concept of size comparison by asking the children to think about the size of different fruit. For instance, consider a pumpkin, a coconut, an orange, a grape, and a blueberry.
- Invite the children to pretend to be these fruits, putting themselves in order from smallest to largest. Then have them try largest to smallest.
- Have the children pretend they are doing the following "fruity" activities:
  - Pick apples
  - Pick strawberries
  - Lift a pumpkin
  - Peel a banana
  - Slice a banana
  - Suck on a lemon!
- Most challenging is pretending to be the following:
  - An orange being peeled
  - A lemon being squeezed
  - A slice of banana floating in a bowl of cereal
  - Apple juice being poured
  - A coconut falling from a tree
  - A grape rolling across the floor!

Read *Eating the Alphabet: Fruits and Vegetables from A to Z* by Lois Ehlert and *I Eat Fruit* by Hannah Tofts and Rupert Horrox.

Frank Leto's *Time for Music* includes a song about fruit called "Let's Go to Market." *Yummy Yummy* by The Wiggles includes "Fruit Salad."

The Human Body

Fun with Grains

The grains group includes such foods as rice, spaghetti, and bread. Besides the fact that they are all grains, these foods have something else in common; they undergo significant changes when cooked. This activity gives the children an opportunity to explore these changes.

To Have

Pastas in different shapes, cooked and uncooked

Rice, cooked and uncooked

Bread and bread dough

To Do

● Show the children a piece of spaghetti. Have the children describe how it looks before it is cooked. Next, show them a strand of cooked spaghetti. Explain that spaghetti gets soft and "wiggly" once it is placed in hot water.

● Show the children samples of cooked and uncooked rice. Explain that rice gets plumper and softer when it is cooked.

● Show children bread and bread dough. Explain that dough gets larger and firmer when it is baked.

● Invite the children to pretend they are each of these foods being cooked and going through changes.

More to Do

● Show the children pastas of varying shapes (for example, shells, bowtie, lasagna, and penne) and ask them to show you these different shapes with their bodies.

Share the book *Bread, Bread, Bread* by Ann Morris. Also read *Everybody Bakes Bread* and *Everybody Cooks Rice* by Norah Dooley.

Rick Charette's *Alligator in the Elevator* includes a song called "Pancakes."

I Love My Teeth!

In this activity, children learn more about teeth, and they find out how important it is to care for their own teeth.

To Have

No materials needed

To Do

- Talk to the children about their teeth. Explain that people start out with baby teeth. These teeth come out to make room for grown-up teeth. Then, people keep their grown-up teeth for their whole lives. That is why people need to take good care of their teeth.
- Next, invite the children to demonstrate some things that people do to take care of their teeth:
  - The shape of a toothbrush
  - The shape of floss
  - The motion of floss sliding between the teeth
  - A tube of toothpaste being squeezed
  - A tube of toothpaste being rolled up from the bottom
  - Electric toothbrush vibrating
  - Brushing teeth!

Share some of these books with the children: *My Tooth Is About to Fall Out* by Grace Maccarone, *Have You Ever Seen a Moose Brushing His Teeth?* by Jamie McClaine, and *Does a Lion Brush?* by Fred Ehrlich.

Play "Brush Your Teeth" from Raffi's *Singable Songs for the Very Young* or another song called "Brush Your Teeth" from *Music Makes It Memorable* by Maryann "Mar" Harman.

The Human Body 35

Introduces the five food groups and promotes awareness of nutrition

Food Groups

With this activity, the children pretend to be foods from the five food groups.

To Have

Pictures of food items from all five food groups

To Do

- Show the children pictures of foods from each of the five food groups: proteins, grains, fruits, vegetables, and dairy.
- Take one food group at a time, and ask the children to pretend they are items that belong to that group. For example, if you are discussing dairy, ask the children to show you what they would look like if they were milk being poured, a piece of string cheese, or a container of yogurt. Can they think of any other items that belong in the group? Continue with the four remaining food groups.

More to Do

- Divide the children into five groups and assign each a food group. The children within that group depict appropriate foods or drinks, either one at a time, with the rest of the children guessing what they are, or together as a group. For example, they might form a bunch of grapes or a plate of spaghetti!
- Divide the children into groups of five, with each child depicting something from a different food group. Can they create a well-balanced meal?

The book *Food Fight* by Carol Diggory Shields provides a silly look at food that children will love. Other book possibilities include: *Gregory the Terrible Eater* by Mitchell Sharmat and *Good Enough to Eat: A Kid's Guide to Food and Nutrition* by Lizzy Rockwell.

Ella Jenkins sings "Let's Not Waste the Food We Eat" on *Come Dance by the Ocean* and Rick Charette includes "Late at Night When I'm Hungry" on *Bubble Gum.*

CHAPTER 2

The Five Senses

Although the senses technically fall under the heading of the human body, the exploration of the senses is extensive enough to warrant a separate chapter.

Like the heart, muscles, and lungs, the senses are not visible to children. The body parts involved in touching, tasting, hearing, smelling, and seeing are visible and concrete; but the senses themselves are abstract concepts and, therefore, require investigation and consideration. You'll find activities here that focus on each sense separately as well as those that utilize and explore all of them. The latter provide the opportunity for children to compare and contrast , thereby offering experience with additional scientific concepts.

The activities in this chapter, along with all the other sensory experiences you present to children, contribute to children's appreciation for the wonderful workings of their bodies.

Head, Shoulders, Knees, & Toes

This body-part identification game requires children to listen carefully as they move from body part to body part. Because listening is related to the sense of hearing, yet another aspect of science is involved.

To Have

No materials needed

To Do

- As you call out "head," "shoulders," "knees," and "toes," children touch the corresponding part of their bodies. First, follow the order of the title, and then mix it up! **Note:** Children are extremely flexible but they should still keep their knees slightly bent when they reach down to touch their toes.

More to Do

- Change the tempo at which you call out the body parts, sometimes doing it slowly and sometimes quickly. You can also start very slowly and gradually increase the tempo until the children dissolve into fits of giggles! Use the lyrics of the traditional song:

Head, Shoulders, Knees, and Toes (Traditional)

Head, shoulders, knees, and toes,　　　*And eyes and ears and mouth and nose.*
Knees and toes.　　　*Head, shoulders, knees, and toes,*
Head, shoulders, knees, and toes,　　　*Knees and toes!*
Knees and toes.

- Substitute a sound for the word "head" (for example, a hand clap, a click of the tongue, a foot stomp, or a kissing sound). Tell the children to touch their heads when they hear that sound. With each successive verse, substitute a different sound for one more body part, until you've replaced all four parts with four different sounds. This really emphasizes the sense of hearing!

This song appears on Greg and Steve's *Big Fun* and on Hap Palmer's *Early Childhood Classics: Old Favorites with a New Twist.*

Simon Says

Here's another game that promotes both body-part identification and listening skills. In the traditional version, those children who need the most practice with either of these skills often are the first to be eliminated! You can promote all children's skill development and enjoyment by playing this game without the elimination process.

To Have

No materials needed

To Do

- Organize the children into two groups (forming two lines or two circles). Explain that they should do as you say only when the command is preceded by the words "Simon says." Then, call out commands like the ones below, sometimes saying "Simon says" before the command and sometimes not. If a child moves without Simon's "permission," that child simply relocates from one line or circle to the other. Note: For new (very young) players, say "Simon says" before every challenge.
- "Simon" might make requests like the following:

  - Raise your arms.
  - Touch your toes.
  - Wiggle your nose.
  - Bend and touch your knees.
  - Make a funny face.
  - Touch your head.
  - Touch your shoulders.

  - Stand on one foot.
  - Blink your eyes.
  - Stand up tall.
  - Pucker up your lips.
  - Put hands on hips.
  - Reach for the sky.
  - Give yourself a hug!

More to Do

- As children become more adept at this game, increase the difficulty by increasing the tempo at which you call out the challenges. Expect lots of laughs!

Have fun with Frank Let's version of "Simon Says" on *Move Your Dancing Feet*.

I Spy

This popular game, played for generations, focuses on the sense of sight. It can be played anywhere—the classroom, the car, or outdoors! Depending on what you're "spying," you can use this game to promote emergent literacy (see More to Do, below), math (also see below), or color recognition, as in the main activity.

To Have

No materials needed

To Do

- Tell the children "I spy something [red]." The children then point to, move to, or touch something they see in that color. Repeat with other colors with which they're familiar.

More to Do

- In addition to colors, you can also spy objects with varying textures, promoting the awareness of the sense of touch.
- Play this game outside to draw attention to nature's wonders!
- Tell the children "I spy something that begins with the [ba] sound," or "I spy something that starts the same way that *dog* does." Repeat with other letters or letter sounds with which the children are familiar.
- Tell the children "I spy something [round; square]."

Jean Marzollo and Walter Wick have created an entire series of *I Spy* books!

Jingle Bells

Young children are fascinated with the sounds created by musical instruments. In this activity, they themselves become the musical instruments!

To Have

One set of jingle bands (Velcro straps with bells attached) per child

To Do

- Once the children have placed the jingle bands on their wrists, invite them to discover different ways they can move to create sounds. Can they make different sounds with the bells?
- Encourage them to find ways to make both soft and loud sounds.

More to Do

- When the children are comfortable with this concept, ask them to find ways first to make continuous sound and, later, sound with pauses in it.

JINGLE BELL

HAND BELL

COW BELL

BELL FROM HOTEL COUNTER

WRIST and ANKLE BELLS

Body Sounds

In the previous activity, the children used a sound-maker—bells. In this activity, the children create sounds using only their bodies.

To Have

No materials needed

To Do

- Stand with the children in a circle and make a sound with a body part (for example, clapping your hands, stomping your feet, chomping your teeth, or smacking your lips).
- The child next to you makes the same sound, and so on all the way around the circle.
- Begin another round with a different sound.

More to Do

- When the children are ready for the responsibility, allow them to take turns starting each round.

Me & My Senses

This simple activity promotes active listening (placing it under the content area of literacy), while offering the opportunity for children to consider the body parts involved with their senses.

To Have

No materials needed

To Do

- Say the following sentences and point to the appropriate body part(s). Have the children complete the sentences by also pointing to the appropriate body part and calling out their answers. They should follow each response with a demonstration of what the sense in action looks like. For example, after "I hear with my [ears]," they might cup a hand to an ear to demonstrate listening.
  - I see with my _____.
  - I hear with my _____
  - I smell with my _____.
  - I taste with my _____.
  - I touch with my _____.

More to Do

- Once children are successful at this activity, eliminate the pointing to make this an active listening activity.

Promotes awareness of the sense of hearing

A Listening Walk

Going on a listening walk gives children the opportunity to focus on the sense of hearing while also getting some much-needed physical activity of moderate to vigorous intensity! Additionally, it offers children a chance to appreciate their natural surroundings.

To Have

No materials needed

To Do

- Take the children on a walk, explaining that they are to listen very carefully as they walk, noting all the different sounds they hear. Remind them to put on their "listening ears" and to move quietly.
- Depending on the children's level of development, you can either ask them to tell you what they're hearing as you walk (least challenging) or wait until you get back to the classroom and ask them to describe all that they heard (more challenging).

More to Do

- Bring a small tape recorder with you. Then play the recording in the classroom and challenge the children to identify the sounds.
- The children portray each identified object, either by taking on its shape or performing its movement. For example, after hearing leaves rustling in the breeze, one child might form the shape of a leaf with her body or body parts. Another child might pretend to be a leaf shaking in the wind.

The Listening Walk by Paul Showers is the perfect accompaniment for these activities.

A Seeing Walk

Children see things wherever they go. This activity, however, requires them to really take note of what they're seeing and, perhaps, not to take their sense of sight for granted.

To Have

Nothing needed

To Do

- Take the children on a walk, explaining that they are to watch very carefully as they walk, noting all the different things they see.
- Depending on the children's level of development, you can either ask them to tell you what they're seeing as you walk (least challenging) or wait until you get back to the classroom and ask them to describe all that they saw (more challenging).

More to Do

- Ask the children to portray each identified object, either by taking on its shape or performing its movement. For example, after seeing someone mail a letter at a mailbox, one child might form the shape of the mailbox with his body. Another child might pretend to be the letter sliding down the chute.

Promotes awareness of the senses

The Five Senses

This activity takes a look at all five senses, creating an opportunity for the children to consider the important functions of the body parts involved.

To Have

No materials needed

To Do

- Talk to the children about the five senses—sight, smell, touch, hearing, and taste—and the body parts involved in each.
- Explain that when you say "sight," they should point to their eyes. When you say "smell," they should point to their nose; and so on. For "taste," they can stick out their tongue and point to it.
- Call out the names of the senses—slowly and in the same order at first. As the children become familiar with the game, you can pick up your tempo and mix up the order!

More to Do

- A more challenging version is to call out the body part and have the children show you its function. When you call out "eyes," they place a hand to the forehead and pretend to be looking for something. For "nose," they sniff the air. For "hands," they pretend to pat something or stroke an arm or cheek. For "ears," they cup an ear with a hand. And for "tongue," they lick their lips.

Read Aliki's *My Five Senses* or *The Five Senses* by Keith Faulkner.

Mar's Playing and Learning with Music includes a song called "Five Senses." "Five Senses" is also a song on Frank Leto's *Time for Music.*

Watch It!

Because chiffon scarves are colorful and tend to float, they make visual tracking easier, meaning they're the perfect prop for successful throwing and catching, and for helping children consider the importance of watching carefully.

To Have

Chiffon scarves (1 per child)

To Do

- Talk to the children about how they need to watch objects very carefully—following them with their eyes—so they can catch an object (in this case, a scarf) successfully!
- Demonstrate how to do this. Throw a scarf up into the air, watch it carefully as it falls, and then catch it.
- Invite each child to toss their scarf into the air and try to catch it.

More to Do

- Challenge the children to discover how many different body parts they can use to catch the scarf. Possibilities include the head, an arm, an elbow, a knee, or a foot.

Hear It!

Being outside means hearing different things! These activities provide an opportunity for children to focus on sound in a natural setting.

To Have

Sturdy twigs or wooden rhythm sticks (1 per child)

To Do

- Bring the children outside and simply ask them to move around the area using their twig or rhythm stick to create different sounds. For example, they might tap a tree trunk in different spots, with various degrees of force and using different parts of their twig or rhythm stick. How different does it sound to rub the tree trunk with the stick? To tap or rub the ground? To move the stick through a pile of leaves?

More to Do

- Challenge the children to stand very still and to be very quiet. After a moment, tell them what you heard—for example, a bird, the leaves rustling in the wind, a bee, or a squirrel. Ask the children to listen for it, too, and then to pretend to be whatever it is they were listening to.

You might accompany these activities with *Listen, Listen*, written by Phillis Gershator.

Touch It!

Children learn so much through their senses, and being outdoors offers a myriad of sensory experiences. This activity will help children consider their sense of touch and simultaneously create an awareness of natural wonders.

To Have

No materials needed

To Do

- With the children scattered about the outside area, call out "Touch something rough." The children then run to touch something rough, like a tree trunk or a rock.
- Continue with different textures, such as *smooth*, *bumpy*, or *slippery*. Repeat each texture more than once so children can consider multiple possibilities for each one.

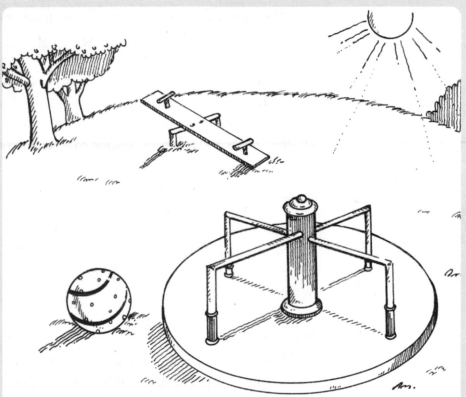

More to Do

- To combine the senses of touch and sight, call out, "Touch something green!" and so forth.

To See or Not to See

This activity challenges the children to consider sight by experiencing its opposite: sightlessness.

To Have

No materials needed

To Do

- The children sit in their own personal space and, after a moment, close their eyes. Ask if it feels any different to have their eyes closed. Invite them to briefly open their eyes to reorient themselves, then close their eyes again and stand up (keeping eyes closed).
- Once the children are standing, ask them to open their eyes for a moment and then close them again. Does standing with eyes closed feel different?
- Continue in this way, cueing the children to experience the differences with their eyes open and then closed when doing the following:
  - Standing on tiptoe
  - Standing (flat-footed) on one foot
  - Standing (briefly) on one foot on tiptoe
  - Standing flat-footed and leaning, alternately, in all four directions; repeat on tiptoe
  - Taking a couple of steps forward, backward, and to either side

More to Do

- Play a game of Sitting in the Dark, in which you arrange chairs in a circle, facing outward, or in one or two lines (facing in opposite directions), with at least 12" of space between them. Ask the children to stand in front of a chair and close their eyes. Then, issue directions such as "Take three steps forward," or "Take two jumps forward." The children do as directed and then reverse the process—without opening their eyes or turning around—and try to get back to their chairs and sit down.

Book possibilities include Dr. Seuss's *The Eye Book*!

Follow That Scent

The smell of yummy food may well be the scent most familiar to young children. This activity gives them an opportunity to consider it.

To Have

One ribbon stick
Soft, slow music

To Do

- Talk to the children about the scent of yummy food in the air and how it makes you want to follow it to find its source. You might use the smell of popcorn popping or cookies baking as examples. How do they think that scent would look if they could see it floating through the air?
- Ask the children to imagine the ribbon is the scent of yummy food, and tell them that they are going to follow it around the room.
- Put on the music and, trailing the ribbon behind you, lead the children throughout the room, inviting them to move as though they were smelling something yummy and following it.

More to Do

- Once the children are familiar with the concept of a scent floating through the air, put on soft, slow music and invite them to move as though *they* were the scent.

Promotes awareness of the sense of hearing

Let's Listen

These next few activities inspire the children to consider the senses, but they also require that the children determine and express their feelings toward the items they're sensing!

To Have

Noise-making items (see below)

To Do

- Invite the children to move in whatever way the sounds make them feel like moving. (Be sure to point out the different responses so the children know it's okay to find their own way.) You might make sounds like the following:
  - Striking a pot with a wooden spoon
  - Ringing a bell
  - Blowing a whistle
  - Shaking a maraca or coffee can partially filled with sand
  - Tapping a desk or wall with a pencil
  - Banging a drum

More to Do

- Inspire movement responses using only body sounds. You might clap, stamp, whistle, cluck your tongue, snap your fingers, smack your lips, pat a thigh, or inhale and exhale loudly. Be sure the children understand that they are to move in the way the sounds make them feel like moving and not to simply imitate what you're doing.

Accompany these activities with *Sounds All Around* by Wendy Pfeffer.

Let's Touch

In this activity, which is a modified version of the traditional "feely-box" game, the children will touch items consisting of various textures and express their responses to them through movement. You may have to help them find the right words for what they're feeling, but that's okay; it's the physical self-expression that matters most.

To Have

Several items, all with a different "feel" (see below)

To Do

- Gather your items together and place them in a large box. Possibilities for a variety of textures include a feather, a teddy bear, a marble or stone, and a piece of silk, burlap, or flannel.
- The children take turns reaching into the box and touching only one item. Can they identify what they're feeling? What does the texture make them think of? How does it make them feel like moving? Invite them to show you! (As an example, a feather might make them feel ticklish; a piece of burlap might make them want to scratch; and a piece of silk might make them feel "slippery.")

DK Publishing has produced a number of *Touch-and-Feel books* that you could use to extend this activity.

Paper Music

This problem-solving activity in which children create sound requires careful listening, making it also an experience in music and literacy.

To Have

One 8½" x 11" sheet of paper

To Do

- Demonstrate how you can make a sound with a piece of paper; for example, by flicking it with a finger or putting a small tear in it.
- Pass the sheet of paper around to the children. Challenge each child to find a way to make a different sound!

Let's Smell

This activity asks the children to interpret and express their feelings about what they're sensing.

To Have

A variety of items with different odors (see below)

To Do

- Gather your items together and arrange them on a table. Possibilities include a flower, an onion, a cookie, and an orange—all of which have distinctive odors.
- Ask each child to choose one item to smell. How does the smell make him feel? Invite him to show you with his face. Can he show you how it makes him feel with his whole body?

More to Do

- Take the children outside to gather items with strong scents!

Book possibilities include *What's That Awful Smell?* by Heather Tekavec and Joanna Cole's *You Can't Smell a Flower with Your Ear!*

Promotes awareness of the sense of taste

Let's Taste

This activity continues the pattern of the last three. This one requires physical self-expression of the sense of taste!

To Have

A variety of items with different flavors (see below)

To Do

- Gather together food items with distinctive flavors and lay them out on a table. Possibilities include lemonade, a pickle, peanut butter, and chocolate.
- Ask each child to choose one item to taste. How does the taste make him feel? Invite him to show you with his face. Can he show you how it makes him feel with his whole body?

More to Do

- Ask the children to show you how "yummy" looks with their face, hands, and whole body. How about "yucky?" Alternate between the two, ending with "yummy!"

Book possibilities include *You Can't Taste a Pickle with Your Ear* by Harriet Ziefert, Leslie Patricelli's *Yummy Yucky*, and *Yummy Yummy, Food for My Tummy* by Sam Lloyd.

Playing the Glasses

This musical activity requires children to listen keenly to the different pitches created.

To Have

Set of water glasses
Water
Pencil

To Do

- Fill the glasses with varying levels of water.
- Let each child take a turn tapping the glasses, listening to see whether the sound each glass makes (the pitch) is lower or higher than the previous one.
- When the children have had ample experience creating the sounds, invite those children who are sitting and listening to move their arms higher or lower, depending on whether the pitch they heard was higher or lower.

CHAPTER 3

Animals & Other Creatures

Young children are fascinated by animals, insects, arachnids, and pretty much all creatures that don't fall into the category of *human*. And because they're so appealing, these creatures are particularly relevant to children.

Moving like different creatures can contribute not only to knowledge about them but also to the development of empathy, an essential component of the social/emotional domain. By imagining what it's like to *be* the animals, children will perhaps never be able to imagine a world *without* the animals.

Of course, moving like different animals and creatures also offers children opportunities to become familiar with a variety of movement skills and elements. If that's to happen, however, it's not enough merely to ask the children to pretend to be various creatures. You must create a greater awareness by discussing pertinent characteristics of the creatures they're portraying. Cats, for example, can move very slowly and quietly. What is it about the way they use their muscles and paws that makes this possible? What is it about their spines that makes them able to twist, stretch, and arch so easily?

The topics in this chapter fall under the heading of life sciences.

Promotes awareness of spiders

The Eensy-Weensy Spider

This old favorite invites children to consider spiders, as well as rain and sunshine. Talk about all of these elements with the children before beginning. How do spiders move? Do they know what a waterspout is? How do they think the sun dries up the rain?

To Have

No materials needed

To Do

- Invite the children to accompany you as you sing and act out the words:

The Eensy-Weensy Spider (Traditional)
The eensy-weensy spider went up the waterspout. (creep your fingers upward)
Down came the rain and washed the spider out. (show falling rain with your hands)
Out came the sun and dried up all the rain. (use your arms to form shape of sun above the head)
And the eensy-weensy spider went up the spout again. (creep fingers upward once more)

More to Do

- Invite the children to show you with their whole bodies how spiders move. Can they show you what it would look like to weave a web? What would they look like if *they* were the web?

The Eensy Weensy Spider, by Mary Ann Hoberman, offers the traditional lyrics as well as some additional adventures for the spider. The children might also enjoy *Diary of a Spider* by Doreen Cronin or *The Very Busy Spider* by Eric Carle.

Hap Palmer's *Early Childhood Classics*; Bob McGrath's *Sing Along with Bob, Volume I*; and Maryann Harman's *Playing and Learning with Music* all include versions of this classic song.

Animal Sounds

Pretending to be animals gives children an opportunity to consider the various creatures that share our world. Learning about the animal kingdom is an important part of life science. Learning about sound is part of physical science. This activity also promotes listening skills.

To Have

Recording of animal sounds

To Do

- Play animal sounds or make them yourself. Here are some to consider:
  - Elephant
  - Horse
  - Gorilla
  - Coyote
  - Lion
  - House cat
  - Dog
  - Mouse
  - Rooster
  - Songbird
  - Rabbit (Just wiggle your nose and be silent.)
- After each sound, ask the children to identify the animal that made it.
- Encourage the children to move the way the animal moves. Give them plenty of time to explore before starting another animal sound.

Share the book *My Very First Book of Animal Sounds* by Eric Carle.

Hap Palmer's *Animal Antics* explores animal sounds and movements. The song "Animal Sounds" on Maryann Harman's *Playing and Learning with Music* gives children a chance to mimic animal sounds.

Animals & Other Creatures

Four-Legged Friends

The two most common—and popular—of our four-legged friends are cats and dogs. This activity allows children to pretend to be each of these animals and encourages them to consider the similarities and differences.

To Have

No materials needed

To Do

- Dogs and cats both move on all four legs.
- Ask the children first to pretend to be dogs and then be cats. Do they move differently?
- Next, invite them to show you how a big, heavy dog "clomps" along. How does a cat move when trying to sneak up on a bird?
- Challenge the children to show you the following movements. Discuss and compare each of them.
  - A dog chasing a stick / a cat pouncing
  - A dog burying a bone / a cat playing with a toy
  - A dog wagging its tail / a cat rubbing against someone
  - A dog rolling over / a cat arching its back
  - A dog sitting up / a cat curling up to go to sleep

Share Norma Simon's *Cats Do, Dogs Don't*, which contrasts the many differences between dogs and cats. Another fun choice just about cats is *The Kitty Cat Alphabet Book* by Andrea Burris and Anna Schad.

Play "My Kitty Cat" and "Floppy Doggy" from Hap Palmer's *Animal Antics*.

The Tortoise & the Hare

The fable of the tortoise and the hare helps children think about differences and similarities between animals. Acting out these differences and similarities helps make them more real to children.

To Have

Pictures of a tortoise and a hare (or rabbit)

To Do

- Talk to the children about tortoises and hares and their characteristics.
- Invite the children to move like each of these animals.
- Divide the group in half, with one group moving like tortoises and one like rabbits. After a while, have the children switch roles.

More to Do

- Read *The Tortoise and the Hare* aloud, inviting the children to act out the story as you read.
- If you have "body socks," sheets, or large towels available, the children can pretend to be tortoises going in and out of their shells.

There are many versions of *The Tortoise and the Hare*, as well as adaptations, to share with the children.

Hap Palmer's *Animal Antics* includes the songs "The Turtle" and "Rabbit Moves Fast." *More Music with Mar* includes a song called "The Turtle."

Promotes awareness of animals

Nuts!

Squirrels build their nests in trees and, when winter is coming, begin to store nuts from trees. In this activity, the children will pretend to be squirrels finding nuts and bringing them back to their nests!

To Have

Several containers filled with Styrofoam peanuts (or something similar)
Small (empty) containers (1 per child)
Lively music

To Do

- Place the filled containers throughout the room.
- Each child stands next to an empty container, which are scattered around the periphery of the room.
- Remind the children that they are squirrels, that their containers represent their trees, *and* that they have to remember where their trees are located!
- When you start the music, the children move around the room pretending to be squirrels hunting for nuts.
- When the music stops, the squirrels move to the nearest container filled with "nuts," take one, and run with it back to their "tree," where they leave it.
- When the music starts again, they repeat the process.

Among the books about squirrels is Nancy Tafuri's *The Busy Little Squirrel*. Lois Ehlert has also created *Nuts to You!*

Jump!

Once children have had the experience of comparing rabbits to tortoises, they will have greater appreciation for the comparison of other animals. In this activity, children compare animals that jump: frogs, rabbits, and kangaroos. This activity also introduces the concept of size comparison.

To Have

Pictures of frogs, rabbits, and kangaroos (optional)

To Do

- Talk to the children about the differences and similarities among frogs, rabbits, and kangaroos. What is the biggest similarity? (Answer: They all jump.) What is one big difference? (Answer: Their size.)
- Encourage each of the children to move like frogs, then rabbits, then kangaroos. Do they jump differently? You may also wish to use the words *hop, jump, leap,* and *bound.*
- Divide the class into three groups. Have the first group be frogs, the second group be rabbits, and the final group be kangaroos. After a while, have the children switch roles.

More to Do

- Play Leap Frog. With the children in a circle—crouched on their hands and feet and facing someone else's back—designate one child to start as the "frog." The "frog" leaps over the child in front of her by placing her hands on the child's back for support. She does the same for each child in front of her until she returns to her original spot in the circle. At that point, the child behind her becomes the next "frog."

Boing! by Nick Bruel tells the story of a young kangaroo, and there's a rabbit in it, too. Other books include *A Frog Thing* (book and CD) by Eric Drachman and *Animals, Animals* by Laura Whipple and Eric Carle.

The children can perform this activity to the instrumental song "Rabbits & 'Roos" by Richard Gardzina, which is available on Rae Pica's *Moving & Learning Series: Preschoolers & Kindergartners.* The children may also enjoy "Jumping Frog" from Hap Palmer's *Pretend.* "Mr. Froggy's Family" takes listeners from tadpoles to full-grown frogs, and is available on Maryann Harman's CD by the same name.

Animals & Other Creatures

Riding the Range

A gallop has an uneven rhythm. It is a combination walk and run, with one foot leading and the other playing catch-up. Galloping like horses allows the children to practice their locomotor skills. Some of the children in your group may not be able to gallop correctly. If that's the case, simply ask the children to pretend to be horses and let them come up with something of their own.

To Have

Music with a 2/4 meter or a drum and beater

To Do

- Play the music or beat out the rhythm of a gallop.
- Invite the children to gallop as if they are horses in an open field.
- Occasionally, pause the music or drumbeat so the "horses" can stop to eat grass. Vary the length of time for both galloping and eating.

More to Do

- Once the children have experienced success leading with their preferred foot, encourage them to lead with the other foot.

Share Laura Driscoll's *Horses* or *The Girl Who Loved Wild Horses* by Paul Goble.

Play the song "Giddy-Up," which is part of Rae Pica's *Moving & Learning Series: Preschoolers & Kindergartners*. The children may also enjoy "Go, Horse, Go," from *Music with Mar & Friends*.

Farm Friends

Many of today's children have never been to a farm, but through books and movies they are generally aware of most common farm animals. Talk about the animals listed below, and compare their physical traits, sounds, and movements.

To Have

Pictures of farm animals (optional)

To Do

- Following your discussion, invite the children to pretend to be a chicken, a duck, a cow, or a horse.

More to Do

- Invite the children to pretend they are more "challenging" animals, such as pigs, goats, sheep, or turkeys.
- Use the animals' sounds to signal the children to move like a particular animal. For example, ask them to begin moving around the area in whatever way they wish. When you call out "Cluck-cluck!" they move like chickens. When you call out "Moo" they move like cows, and so forth. This is a great auditory discrimination activity.
- Sing and act out "Old MacDonald Had a Farm" and/or "The Farmer in the Dell."
- Play Ducks, Cows, Cats, & Dogs. With this game, you whisper the name of an animal into each child's ear. When all children have been assigned an animal, they get on hands and knees, close their eyes, and begin moving about the area, making the sound of their animal. The goal is for each "animal" to find its own kind—just by listening. When all of the animals of one kind have found one another, have them stop and watch the remaining animals search.

Share *The Year at Maple Hill Farm*, written by Alice and Martin Provensen, with the children. Other possibilities include Lois Ehlert's *Color Farm* or *Sounds on the Farm* by Gail Donovan.

"The Farmer in the Dell" and "Mary Had a Little Lamb" are part of Ella Jenkins's *Early, Early Childhood Songs*. "The Farmer Feeds Us" and is available on *Ella Jenkins and a Union of Friends Pulling Together*.

Animals & Other Creatures 67

Creepy Creatures

Whether slithering on their bellies or stalking prey, the animals explored in this activity all move very close to the ground.

To Have

Pictures of such animals as snakes, lizards, chameleons, alligators, and seals (optional)

To Do

- Talk to the children about these animals and their characteristics.
- Encourage the children to show you how each of the creatures would move.

More to Do

- When the children are ready for cooperative work, help them pair off. Have them stretch out on their bellies, one child in front of the other. The child in the back takes hold of the ankles of the child in front, forming a two-person "snake" or "eel." Can the children slither together without coming apart?
- The next challenge is for each two-person snake or eel to connect with other two-person creatures, until they all form one big creature.
- Play Tail of the Snake. Have the children line up, each with their hands on the hips of the child in front. At your signal, the player in front (the head of the snake) tries to tag the player at the back of the line (the tail of the snake)— without causing the snake to come apart. If the snake does come apart, the children should quickly try to put it back together again. If the player in front is able to catch the snake's tail, she goes to the back of the line and becomes the tail for the next round.

Read *Can Snakes Crawl Backward?* by Melvin and Gilda Berger, or *Snakes, Salamanders, and Lizards* by Diane L. Burns.

The Elephant

Children are especially fascinated by large animals, and elephants are the largest land animals. Human intrusion has significantly reduced their numbers. Perhaps activities like this will create an appreciation and concern for elephants.

To Have

A piece of slow, "heavy" music

Picture of an elephant (optional)

To Do

- The elephant is probably best known for its size and its unusual nose, which is called a *trunk*. Talk to the children about elephants.
- Then ask the children to show you how an elephant swings, eats with, and showers with its trunk!
- Put on the piece of music, inviting the children to move around the area like elephants.
- When you pause the music the children should perform one of the above three activities.

Share Jerry Smath's *But No Elephants* with the children.

Introduces prehistoric animals and reinforces math concepts

Dinosaur Stomp

*This activity involves a kind of creature that fascinates children: dinosaurs.
It also provides an opportunity to work with the math concepts of weight
and size.*

To Have

Hand drum and beater
Illustrations of dinosaurs (optional)

To Do

● Talk with the children about dinosaurs. Are they big or small? Light or heavy?
How much do the children think dinosaurs weigh? Explain that very large
dinosaurs might weigh as much as a bus! Finally, discuss how a big, heavy
animal like a dinosaur might walk.

● Strike the drum with slow, heavy beats, and invite the children to pretend to be
dinosaurs walking to this rhythm. (**Note:** Matching an imposed rhythm is
developmentally challenging, so do not worry if the children do not move at
one with the beat.) Continue in this manner, encouraging the "dinosaurs" to
vary their paths (straight, curving, and zigzagging) and occasionally changing
the tempo of the beats to be a bit slower or quicker.

More to Do

● When the children are comfortable with this activity, ask them to demonstrate
how a big, heavy dinosaur would run. How would a dinosaur dance? Follow this
by asking how a big, heavy dinosaur would lie down.

● Play a game of Kitty Cat & Dinosaur. This activity has children comparing the
movements of something that is small and light with something that is big and
heavy. Start by having all the children move like kitty cats. At your signal, have
the children switch and pretend to be dinosaurs. Remind them, if necessary,
that kitty cats move very lightly, especially when they're sneaking up on
something, while dinosaurs lumber along with big, heavy steps.

Saturday Night at the Dinosaur Stomp by Carol Diggory Shields is a great story for
the children to act out. You can also read Paul Strickland's *Dinosaur Stomp!*

The Woodpecker

This simple activity not only creates an awareness of one of the planet's feathered friends, it also provides an opportunity for the children to experience rhythm, which falls under the content areas of music and language arts.

To Have

Picture of a woodpecker (optional)

To Do

- Explain to the children that woodpeckers use their very strong beaks to peck at the bark or wood of trees for two reasons: to drill for insects to eat and to dig holes for their nests. If the children have ever seen or heard a woodpecker pecking at a tree, they know it's very rhythmic and makes a fairly loud sound.

- Tell the children they're going to pretend to be woodpeckers drilling at trees and that they'll "peck" in echoing response to the rhythms you establish. For example, if you clap two times at a slow tempo, each child uses their head to peck two times at the same tempo, saying aloud, "Peck, peck."
- Repeat each pattern at least once.

Reading The Owl and the Woodpecker by Brian Wildsmith can provide an opportunity for comparing and contrasting these two birds.

Hibernate!

In the winter, many animals have less food available to them. Some animals cope with this by "going to sleep" during the cold months. This is called hibernation. *It helps animals save energy when food is hard to find. Although many animals, such as chipmunks, frogs, and ladybugs hibernate, we think most often of bears.*

To Have

Hoop, poly spot, or carpet square (1 per child)

To Do

- Talk to the children about bears. Discuss how they look and move. Use the words *lumbering* (a slow, heavy way of walking) and *slumbering* (sleeping).
- Scatter the "caves" (hoops, spots, or carpet squares) on the floor throughout the room.
- When you say "lumber!" have the children move like bears throughout the area. When you say "slumber!" have the children move toward the closest "cave," lie down, curl up, and go to sleep. When you say "lumber!" once again, the children should slowly awaken and walk about the room.
- Vary the length of time for both lumbering and slumbering.

crawling

curled up

Share the book *Bear Snores On* by Karma Wilson.

Being Bees

In this activity, the children will discover that bees are actually doing important work when they land on flowers. They are dropping little grains of pollen onto the flower so that it can make seeds and grow new plants. At the very least, they will enjoy buzzing around like busy bees!

To Have

Several hoops, poly spots, or carpet squares

"Flight of the Bumblebee," a classical piece by Rimsky-Korsakov (or some other lively music)

To Do

- Scatter the place markers you have chosen. Explain to the children that these markers are the flowers that they will be visiting as "bees."
- Start the music and encourage the children to pretend they are bees flying around. When you pause the music, tell each "bee" to visit the nearest "flower." The "bees" visit by stepping inside a hoop or standing on a poly spot or carpet square.
- Continue the game, starting and stopping the music, as long as the children stay interested. Vary the amount of time between each action so children will not know what to expect.

Share *Buzz-Buzz, Busy Bees* by Dawn Bentley and Melanie Gerth. Other book possibilities include *Are You a Bee?* by Judy Allen and *Buzz Said the Bee* by Wendy Cheyette Lewison.

Frank Leto's *Circle Time* includes a song called "Butterflies and Bumblebees."

Animals & Other Creatures 73

Promotes awareness of insects and invites comparison

Being Bugs

Children typically enjoy watching and playing with bugs. Actually pretending to be a bug can help children develop an even greater appreciation for them. Talk with the children about the various bugs listed below, discussing their differences and similarities.

To Have

Pictures of insects (optional)

To Do

- Invite the children to act like each of these flying insects:
  - Mosquito
  - Bumblebee
  - Butterfly
  - Fly
  - Ladybug
  - Firefly
- Now invite the children to act like each of these crawling insects:
  - Ant
  - Flea
  - Caterpillar
  - Roly-poly pill bug
  - Cricket
  - Inchworm
- You may also have the children act like spiders, but tell them that spiders are not bugs. Bugs have six legs. Spiders have eight. Caterpillars and inchworms are considered bugs because they turn into moths and butterflies that have six legs.

Read Anne Rockwell's *Bugs Are Insects*!

The CD *Insects and Spiders* by the Educational Record Center has 12 songs that can be played to accompany this activity.

Creatures That Swim

From humans to ducks to whales, creatures that swim are a varied group of animals. Talk to the children about the different fish and mammals listed below. Compare how they swim and where they live.

To Have

Pictures of various swimming creatures

To Do

- Invite the children to pretend they are each of these creatures. What do they have in common? They swim mostly on top of the water.
  - Person snorkeling
  - Duck
  - Otter
  - Dog
  - Alligator
- Next, invite the children to pretend they are each of these creatures. What do they have in common? They swim mostly underwater.
  - Person scuba-diving
  - Eel
  - Shark
  - Goldfish
  - Stingray

More to Do

- Play Seaweed Tag. Have one child, acting as "seaweed," stand in the middle of a designated area called the "ocean." Have the rest of the children be the "fish" lined up on one end of the ocean. At your signal, the fish try to cross the ocean. If tagged by the seaweed, they also become seaweed. This means they have to keep one foot planted on the "ocean floor" at all times, but they can bend their bodies and move their arms. Those fish who make it safely to the other side can try to cross again. The game continues until all the fish have become seaweed. The last fish tagged is the first to act as seaweed for the next round.

I'm the Biggest Thing in the Ocean by Keven Sherry tells the story of a squid. Or you might share *Over in the Ocean: In a Coral Reef* by Marianne Berkes.

Play the song "A Hump Back Whale" from *Come Dance by the Ocean* by Ella Jenkins. Georgiana Stewart's *Musical Scarves and Activities* includes a song called "Under the Sea." There's also "Doing the Swim" by Frank Leto on *Steel Band Jamboree.*

Animals & Other Creatures

Promotes awareness of birds and invites comparison

Being Birds

There are so many different species of birds! They come in different colors, different sizes, and different shapes. They make different sounds, and they even move differently. This activity gives children the opportunity to consider these differences and develop an appreciation for all our feathered friends.

To Have

Pictures of a variety of birds

To Do

- Talk to the children about the following actions, which are typical of many kinds of birds, and then invite them to act out the different actions:
  - Flying
  - Landing on a branch
  - Building a nest
  - Feeding a baby bird
  - Bathing in a puddle
- Next, discuss the birds below and the different approaches they have for getting food. Challenge the children to act out the following:
  - A woodpecker clinging to the side of a tree and pecking for insects
  - A robin scratching for worms in the ground
  - A hummingbird hovering at a flower to sip nectar
  - A small bird sitting on a branch and cracking a sunflower seed
  - A heron "fishing" along the shore
  - A pelican diving for a fish
  - A seagull searching for food at the beach

Read *Birds, Nests, and Eggs* by Mel Boring or *How Do Birds Find Their Way?* by Roma Gans.

Hap Palmer's *Animal Antics* includes a song called "Hummingbird," and Ella Jenkins' *Come Dance by the Ocean* has "Bye Bye Sea Birds."

Animals That...

Now that the children have considerable experience considering different kinds of animals and pretending to move like them, they should be ready to classify them!

To Have

No materials needed

To Do

- Talk with the children about all the different animals they have pretended to be. What are some of the things they have in common? What are some of the ways in which they are different? Give the children plenty of time to consider all the responses.
- Next, invite the children to move and sound like an animal that would belong to each of these groups. The children will enjoy guessing what their classmates have become. Encourage the children to differentiate between the animals they are pretending to be based on which of the following the creatures:
  - Walk
  - Run
  - Jump
  - Fly
  - Swim

Share the book *Do Frogs Fly?* by Moira Butterfield.

Promotes awareness of insects and introduces the concept of metamorphosis

Metamorphosis

For butterflies, there are four basic stages in the metamorphosis process: egg, caterpillar, chrysalis, and butterfly. Talk to the children about this process before beginning the activity. Have the children ever heard of a chrysalis? Have they ever seen a chrysalis hanging from a leaf? Have they seen a butterfly egg, a caterpillar, or a butterfly? What did these look like? How did they move?

To Have

Body sock, sheet, or large towel (1 per child)

To Do

- Have the children lie on the floor, each wrapped in their "chrysalis." At your signal, tell the children to begin, very slowly, to "emerge." Have them shed their chrysalis and turn into butterflies, fluttering around the room.
- Tell the children that butterflies get thirsty. Encourage them to pause now and then, pretending to drink nectar from a flower. Ask them how butterflies hold their wings when they land on something. You may want to tell them that butterflies hold their wings up behind them, but moths hold their wings stretched out at their sides.

More to Do

- Explore more stages of metamorphosis, beginning with the caterpillar stage. Have the children move as caterpillars before entering their chrysalises.

Read *From Caterpillar to Butterfly* by Deborah Heiligman or *Are You a Butterfly?* by Judy Allen.

Hap Palmer's *Animal Antics* includes a song called "Butterfly," and Carole Peterson's *Tiny Tunes* includes "Fuzzy Wuzzy Caterpillar/Butterfly."

CHAPTER 4

The Seasons, Weather, & Other Natural Wonders

The intention of this chapter is to help create a greater awareness of the natural elements that are part of the outdoors. Just as children are fascinated by animals, they are captivated by what they can see outside their windows. Enhancing this fascination through experiences with movement, music, and other means, may help children hold onto their love of the outdoors.

Sadly, today's children spend little to no time outside. When children spend most of their time indoors, they're missing out on everything the outdoors has to offer them, including:

- The many sensory experiences children can only have outside.
- Natural light, which stimulates the pineal gland, the part of the brain that helps regulate our biological clock. This gland is vital to the immune system, and simply makes us feel happier. Natural light also triggers the synthesis of Vitamin D and has been shown to increase academic learning and productivity.
- The aesthetic value of the natural world. Because the natural world is filled with amazing sights, sounds, and textures, it's the perfect resource for the development of aesthetics in young children. Because aesthetic awareness means a heightened sensitivity to the beauty around us, it's something that can serve children well for a lifetime.

The activities in this chapter explore such topics as plants, the sun, wind, clouds, temperature, night and day, air resistance, and more. These topics fall under the categories of life, Earth, space, and physical science.

Introduces the concept of air resistance

Scarf Dancing

When children dance with a scarf or streamer, they can actually see air resistance, a concept that falls under the heading of physical science.

To Have

Chiffon scarves or ribbon sticks (1 per child)
Recorded music
Parachute (optional)

To Do

- Play the music and invite the children to see how many ways they can move the scarf or streamer to it. (Focusing on the prop rather than on their own bodies—and using the word *move* rather than *dance*—helps alleviate self-consciousness in shy children.)
- Ask the children to imagine the air pushing against the scarf or streamer to make it move.
- Try music with a different "feel" to inspire different kinds of movement.

More to Do

- Take this activity outside on a windy day (with or without music) so the children can fully experience air resistance!
- Fly a kite!
- Bring the parachute outside and challenge the children to make ripples and waves with it. Invite them to make an "igloo" by raising the parachute high into the air and pulling it quickly back down, trapping air under the parachute. After the children have experienced this a few times, encourage them to raise the parachute as high as they can, and then let go of it and observe what happens.

Read *Air Is All Around You* by Franklyn M. Branley.

Try the creative scarf activities found on *Musical Scarves and Activities* by Georgiana Stewart. Also, try *Streamer and Ribbon Activities* by Henry "Buzz" Glass and Jack Capon.

Forever Blowing Bubbles

When children blow bubbles, they can see the air pushing the liquid out to form a sphere. This is another form of air resistance, which falls under the heading of physical science. And, since children expand and contract their lungs to blow, this activity also creates awareness of lungs.

To Have

Bottle of bubbles (1 per child)

Piece of construction paper or paper fan (1 per child, optional)

To Do

- Invite the children to practice blowing bubbles. Ask them to consider how they can make bigger or smaller bubbles.
- Now encourage the children to make their bubbles go higher by blowing on them. Can they get their bubbles to change direction?

More to Do

- Give each child a paper fan or a piece of construction paper folded in half. Challenge the children to blow a bubble and then try to change the bubble's direction by using the paper or fan.

Read Mercer Mayer's *Bubble Bubble.*

The Seasons, Weather, & Other Natural Wonders

Promotes consideration of trees and shade

Under the Old Oak Tree

One of the things trees are best known for is providing shade, which is especially wonderful on a hot, sunny day.

To Have

No materials needed

To Do

- This game is a variation of Freeze Tag, in which one player is "It" and tagged players must remain frozen, feet apart, until another player crawls under their legs.
- In this game, tagged players must sit until another player comes and, taking the shape of a tree, offers "shade."
- The tagged player can then rejoin the game.
- If "It" manages to tag everybody, the last person sitting gets to be "It" for the next game.

Shel Silverstein's *The Giving Tree* would make a wonderful accompaniment to this activity.

The Four Seasons

This simple, enjoyable activity calls children's attention to the differences among the four seasons. If you live in an area that does not experience seasonal changes, use photos or pictures to help describe the differences.

To Have

No materials needed

To Do

- Explain to the children that they will act out special characteristics of each season when you call them out. For instance, when you call out "summer," the children should pretend to be hot. When you call out "winter," they will show you what it looks like to be cold. When you say "autumn," they can pretend to be falling leaves. Finally, when you say "spring," they should be flowers growing.
- Call out the seasons in the same order at first, at a slow pace. As the children become more experienced with the activity, pick up your pace and mix up the order!

More to Do

- Invite the children to pretend they are doing some of the special activities that people do during each season. Here are some possibilities:
  - Spring—planting a garden, sniffing flowers, spring cleaning, flying a kite, playing in the rain
  - Summer—swimming, surfing, paddling a canoe, building a sand castle, licking an ice cream cone
  - Autumn—raking leaves, jumping in a leaf pile, picking apples, trick-or-treating
  - Winter—skiing, ice skating, building a snowman, having a snowball fight, shoveling snow
- How many other activities can the children think of?

Read *The Reason for Seasons* by Gail Gibbons, or *Skip through the Seasons* by Stella Blackstone.

Listen to the song "Seasons" on Hap Palmer's *Can Cockatoos Count by Twos* or "Months and Seasons" on Vincent's *Working Together*.

The Seasons, Weather, & Other Natural Wonders

Promotes awareness of spring and plant growth

Spring to Life!

Many teachers have children plant seeds in paper cups and watch them grow. This is a wonderful accompaniment to that activity. Children get to pretend that they are the seeds, growing into plants, flowers, and even trees!

To Have

No materials needed

To Do

- Talk to the children about seeds. What grows from seeds? Is there a season when plants start to grow?
- Invite the children to pretend they are seeds by getting into the smallest possible shape on the floor or ground.
- Move throughout the area, pretending that you are the sun and then the rain. As you move, the "seeds" should slowly begin to poke through the soil and grow into whatever they wish. Have the children describe what kind of plant or tree they are.

Read *The Tiny Seed* by Eric Carle or *A Seed Is Sleepy* by Dianna Hutts Aston.

Rick Charette's *Popcorn and Other Songs to Munch On* includes a song called "Plant a Seed." Carole Peterson's *Tiny Tunes* includes "I'm a Little Seed."

Autumn Leaves

In many parts of the country, the leaves on deciduous trees change color in September and October. Eventually, these trees lose their leaves in order to conserve water through the winter. Talk to the children about this process, describing the brilliant colors and the falling leaves. Use movement words such as drifting, floating, *and* swirling.

To Have

Parachute (optional)

Real or paper leaves (optional)

To Do

- Invite the children to pretend they are autumn leaves hanging on the trees. Can they show you what it would look like to move in the breeze? How would they move in a strong wind?
- Next, challenge the children to demonstrate leaves doing the following:
  - Being forced off the trees by very strong wind
  - Gently falling off the trees and floating to the ground
  - Drifting through the air before settling on the ground
  - Swirling around and around in the wind
  - Being lifted higher and lower by the wind
  - Landing gently in a soft pile

More to Do

- Place leaves on a parachute and encourage the children to make them fall to the ground.
- Invite the children to pretend they are raking leaves into a big pile.
- Invite the children to pretend to jump into a pile of leaves and then throw the leaves into the air.
- Take the children outside to gather and play with leaves!

Read *Why Do Leaves Change Color?* by Betsy Maestro or *Red Leaf, Yellow Leaf* by Lois Ehlert.

Rick Charette's *Toad Motel* includes a song called "Falling Leaves."

The Seasons, Weather, & Other Natural Wonders

Goin' on a Treasure Hunt

Children are born collectors, so this activity gives them an excuse to do what comes naturally!

To Have

Small pail or bag (1 per child)
Large container for the group (cardboard box)
Blanket

To Do

- Bring the children outside and simply challenge them to find as many rocks as they can.
- When you give the signal to stop, the children should bring their treasures to a central meeting place and put them on the blanket for all to see. How are the rocks different? How are they the same? Which is the biggest? Which is the strangest?
- Next, have the children collect another kind of treasure. For example, they can search for fallen leaves, twigs, or flower petals.

More to Do

- Once all of the items of one kind have been collected, ask the children to classify them. For example, if the children have been collecting rocks they might organize them according to color, texture, or size.

Share the book *Let's Go Rock Collecting* by Roma Gans.

Let It Snow!

Children are fascinated by snow even if they have never seen it before. This activity provides an opportunity for them to consider snow in a variety of forms.

To Have

Parachute (optional)

Cotton balls (optional)

Black construction paper, one piece per child

To Do

- Invite the children to depict the following with their body or body parts:
  - Snowball
  - Snowball getting bigger and bigger
  - Snowstorm
  - Snowflake shape
  - Snowflake falling
  - Snow person
  - Snow person melting slowly in the sun

More to Do

- Place cotton balls on a parachute and invite the children to create a "snowstorm" by tossing them up into the air.
- Sing and act out or dance to "Frosty the Snowman."
- Ask the children to use the cotton balls to form a snow sculpture.
- If it snows in your area, bring the children outside. Give them each a piece of black construction paper that they can use to catch snowflakes!

Share *White Snow, Bright Snow* by Alvin Tresselt, *The First Snowfall* by Anne Rockwell, or Lois Ehlert's *Snowballs.*

Greg & Steve's *Rockin' Down the Road* includes a song called "Snowflake." Hap Palmer's *Quiet Places* includes "Snowfall." *The Wiggle, Giggle, and Shake CD* by Rae Pica and Richard Gardzina includes "Dance of the Snowflakes."

The Seasons, Weather, & Other Natural Wonders

Creates awareness of the ocean

Ebb Tide

Have the children in your class ever been to the ocean? Talk to them about the ocean's low and high tides and what the waves look like during each. For example, at high tide the waves tend to be larger—roaring in, cresting, and foaming as they approach the beach. During low tide, the waves don't come in as far and they're smaller, rolling in more gently, with just a few bubbles as they reach the sand.

To Have

Large map of the United States (optional)
Dark marker or crayon (optional)

To Do

- Invite the children to move like a wave at low tide.
- Next, ask them to pretend that time is passing and the tide is getting higher. The waves continue to grow until, finally, at high tide, they're as big as they can get.
- If time permits, reverse the process.

More to Do

- Teach the children "the wave," as seen at sporting events.
- Place a large map on the wall and explain to the children that they are going to "walk" the shoreline along the east or west coast. Then, take the children for a walk around the building, classroom, gym, or playground. Every time you go around, use a brightly colored or dark marker to designate on a map a mile "traveled" along the chosen coastline. When you've traversed the entire coastline, start on the other one! This is a great way to promote daily physical activity while offering a lesson in geography and promoting interest in the ocean!

Over in the Ocean: In a Coral Reef, written by Marianne Berkes, would be a great accompaniment to these activities.

"Come Dance by the Ocean" is a song on Ella Jenkins' album of the same name.

Rain, Rain

Rain often gets a "bad rap" because most people prefer sunshine. But there would be no life without rain! Talk to the children about what rain does, including watering plants and vegetables and replenishing bodies of water. Ask the children to tell you what they like best about rainy days.

To Have

Rain sticks

To Do

- Give some children rain sticks, inviting the rest to act as the rain. Have the children act their parts while singing or chanting "Rain, Rain Go Away." The lyrics are as follows:

    Rain, Rain, Go Away (Traditional)
    Rain, rain, go away,
    Come again another day,
    If you don't, I will say,
    Rain, rain go away.

    Rain, rain, go away,
    Come again some other day,
    We want to go outside and play,
    Come again some other day.

- If possible, give all of the children an opportunity to use the rain sticks.

There are plenty of books about rain to share with the children. Among them are *Bringing the Rain to Kapiti Plain* by Verna Aardema; *Come On, Rain*, written by Karen Hesse; and *Down Comes the Rain*, written by Franklyn M. Branley.

The Seasons, Weather, & Other Natural Wonders

Awake & Asleep

The concepts of night *and* day *fall under the heading of Earth and space science. This fun game promotes awareness of the fact that humans are active during the day but asleep at night. It also gives an opportunity to discuss other creatures that have sleeping habits dissimilar from the children. Raccoons, bats, and moths, for instance, are all creatures of the night.*

To Have

No materials needed

To Do

- Talk to the children about being awake during the day and asleep at night. Can they think of any animals that are awake at night?
- Explain to the children that they will pretend to be people going about their busy day. Have them move around the room in any way they want. When you call out "night!" the children collapse to the floor and pretend to be asleep. When you call out "day!" the children pop up and begin moving around the room again.
- Next, invite the children to be night creatures. They are raccoons, bats, or moths going about their nighttime business. When you call out "Day!" the children collapse to the floor and pretend to be asleep. When you call out "Night!" they pop up and begin to move around the room again.

More to Do

- Encourage the children to move in a special way when they are "awake." For example, you might challenge them to jump, march, dance, fly, or flutter.

Read *What Makes Day and Night* by Franklyn M. Branley.

Apples & Pumpkins

In some parts of the country, people pick apples in September and pick pumpkins in October. This activity gives children an opportunity to think about autumn and the fruits that are available at different times of the year. It also gets children to consider opposites such as high and low, heavy and light, and big and small.

To Have

Pictures of an apple tree and a pumpkin patch

Apple and pumpkin (optional)

To Do

- Discuss these fruits with the children. How do people pick them? Encourage the children to pretend they are reaching *high* into the trees for apples and then *low* to the ground for pumpkins.
- Remind the children of the sizes of the fruit. Are apples big or small? What about pumpkins? Also encourage the children to consider the weight of the fruit. Are apples light or heavy? What about pumpkins? Encourage the children to show you what it would look like to pick apples and pumpkins.
- Now, play a fruit-picking game. Call out the name of each fruit, beginning at a slow to moderate tempo. As the children hear the name of each fruit, they pretend to pick it. Eventually, pick up the pace. Even if you go too fast for the children, they will love trying to keep up.

More to Do

- Divide the children into pairs. Assign each child to be either an apple or a pumpkin. Challenge the children to show you the difference in size between these two round fruits.
- Ask children to imagine that they are tiny pumpkin or apple seeds in the ground. As you pretend to be the rain and the sun, the "seeds" slowly start to grow into great, big, round pumpkins or big, beautiful apple trees.

Read *Picking Apples and Pumpkins* by Amy Hutchings; *Apples and Pumpkins* by Anne Rockwell; *It's a Fruit, It's a Vegetable, It's a Pumpkin* by Allan Fowler; or *How Apple Trees Grow* by Joanne Mattern.

Listen to "Way Up High in an Apple Tree" and "Five Little Pumpkins" from Music by Mar's album *Songs at My Fingertips*.

The Seasons, Weather, & Other Natural Wonders

Promotes awareness of the sun

You Are My Sunshine

Learning about the sun—and the Earth's relationship to it—is an important part of Earth science. This activity gives children an opportunity to consider why the sun rises in the same place every day and where it goes every night. Explain that the Earth is turning and as it turns, different parts of the Earth face the sun. Some parts do not. Those parts that face the sun are experiencing day. The parts that face away from the sun are experiencing night.

To Have

No materials needed

To Do

- Begin by asking the children about the sun. What is it made of? Is it hot or cold?
- Encourage the children to pretend they are little suns shining. What would they look like if they were the sunshine?
- Next, ask the children to make themselves into tiny round shapes on the floor. Tell them they are pretending to be the sun about to rise. At your signal, they begin to rise, travel slowly to the opposite side of the activity area, and then slowly set. If time allows, you can repeat this six more times, representing the seven days of the week!

More to Do

- Play a game in which the children smile when you call out "sunshine!" and frown when you say "clouds!"
- Go outside on a sunny day, and invite the children to play Shadow Tag. The child who is "It" has to tag a player by stepping on his shadow. When one child tags another, the tagged child freezes until another player steps on his shadow.
- Encourage the children to see how many different movements they can get their shadows to do!

Read *Sunshine Makes the Seasons* by Franklyn Mansfield Branley or *Sun Up, Sun Down* by Gail Gibbons.

Greg & Steve's *Rockin' Down the Road* includes "Sunshine Medley," and Bob McGrath's *Sing Along with Bob, Vol. 2* includes "You Are My Sunshine."

Running like the Wind

The wind has many "moods." The wind can be a gentle breeze that cools us on a hot day; the wind can be the energy that sails a boat or turns the blades on a windmill; the wind can even be a ferocious storm, bending trees and scattering leaves.

To Have

Ribbon sticks (1 per child)

2 pieces of music: one soft and one more forceful (optional)

To Do

- On a day when there is a good stiff breeze, talk with the children about the wind.
- Bring the children outdoors with their ribbon sticks. Invite them to hold their sticks above their heads and watch what the wind does to the ribbons. How do the ribbons move? Can they imagine what the wind would look like? Can they move their bodies the same way their ribbons move? Ask what happens to the ribbons if they move them back and forth or side to side.
- Invite the children to walk, holding their sticks overhead, and pretend they *are* the wind. What kind of wind are they? A gentle breeze? A strong headwind? A ferocious storm?

More to Do

- Explore the concept of wind indoors. Discuss the difference between a gentle breeze and a strong wind, and then play the two pieces of music. Have the children listen to the music and act out the kinds of winds they each inspire. They can do this with or without ribbon sticks.

Charlotte Zolotow's *When the Wind Stops* answers questions about the wind and other elements of natural science.

Carole Peterson's *Stinky Cake* includes a song called "The Wind."

The Seasons, Weather, & Other Natural Wonders

Creates awareness of clouds

Being Clouds

Passing clouds are fun to watch, but sometimes we forget to take the time. This activity encourages children to pay attention to clouds and appreciate their changing beauty.

To Have

Pictures of different types of clouds

Large dancing scarves (optional)

To Do

- If possible, bring the children outside. Show them the pictures of clouds and ask if they can identify which clouds are in the sky.
- Ask the children which way the cloud is moving. Encourage the children to move like that cloud.
- After a few moments, challenge the children to try to find their cloud again. Is it still the same shape? Can the children make this new shape with their bodies?

More to Do

- Give each child a dancing scarf. Have the children pretend to be clouds drifting in the sky.
- Lie on the ground with the children and encourage them to find creatures in the clouds. Each time a child discovers a "creature," he should get up and move the way that creature would move.

Accompany this activity with a reading of Thomas Locker's *Cloud Dance.*

Hap Palmer's *Quiet Places* includes a song called "Touching Clouds." The CD *Streamer and Ribbon Activities* by Henry Buzz Glass and Jack Capon includes the song "A Soft White Cloud."

Wonders of the Sky

The sky seems mysterious and unknowable to young children, but this activity will give them occasion to consider its mysteries and even pretend to be parts of the sky.

To Have

No materials needed

To Do

- Talk to the children about the following:
  - A twinkling star
  - The shape of a star
  - The sun
  - A full moon
  - A half moon
  - A rainbow
- Now ask them to show you what each would look like!

 You may want to read *The Sky Is Full of Stars* by Franklyn M. Branley or *The Kids' Book of the Night Sky* by Ann Love and Jane Drake.

The Seasons, Weather, & Other Natural Wonders

Promotes awareness of weather

Weathering the Storm

Children are fascinated, and sometimes frightened, by various kinds of weather. This activity gives children the opportunity to be different kinds of weather. Maybe if a child pretends to be a loud thunderstorm, he will feel less afraid the next time Mother Nature unleashes her fury!

To Have

No materials needed

To Do

- Invite the children to show you what they would look like if they were the following:
  - Dark storm clouds
  - Wind, blowing hard
  - Pouring rain
  - Light drizzle
  - Fog
  - Hail
  - Thunder
  - Lightning

More to Do

- When the children are ready to handle the responsibility of cooperative participation, assign some to be the clouds, others to be the wind, and so forth. Have them create an entire "storm" in your classroom or on the playground!
- Play a game of Thunder & Lightning. The children split up into partners. One partner is Thunder. The other is Lightning. At your signal, the partners separate and begin moving around the room, keeping their eyes on one another. Each time "Lightning" decides to strike (by moving any way he wishes to show lightning), thunder must follow with an action of his own (because thunder follows lightning). After a while, the partners reverse roles.

Read *Weather Words and What They Mean* by Gail Gibbons. Other possibilities are *Flash, Crash, Rumble, and Roll* and *Down Comes the Rain*, both by Franklyn M. Branley.

Try playing "Weather Song" on *All Day Long with Dr. Jean*.

Water & Ice

This activity is a great way to introduce the concept of freezing to children. Explain that water gets hard and freezes when it is cold enough. When water gets warm enough, it melts. When water gets really hot, the opposite of cold, it turns into steam!

To Have

Outdoor thermometer
Paper plates (2 per child, optional)

To Do

- Before beginning, talk about the red line on the thermometer. Explain that puddles, ponds, and lakes will turn to ice when temperatures get cold enough (usually in winter). These bodies of water melt again when the temperatures get warm enough.
- Have the children split up into pairs. In each pair, one child gets to be the thermometer while the other child gets to be the puddle. Begin the game with the "thermometer" standing. This means it is hot outside because the "thermometer" is as "high" as it can get. Now, have the "thermometer" lower by slowing falling to the floor. At this point, the child who is the "puddle" slowly stands up, turning himself into ice and getting harder. Have the "thermometer" rise again so that the "puddle" melts once more. Next, have the children reverse roles.

More to Do

- If the children are not ready to split up into pairs, you can act as the thermometer, with all of the children pretending to be puddles and ice around you.
- Invite the children to pretend to be icicles or giant ice sculptures, slowly melting in the sun.

Read *Angelina Ice Skates* by Katharine Holabird or *Callie Cat, Ice Skater* by Eileen Spinelli. You can further explore the concept of temperature by reading Melissa Gish's *Temperature*.

Accompany either of the last two activities with a Johann Strauss waltz or Emil Waldteufel's "Skater's Waltz."

The Seasons, Weather, & Other Natural Wonders

CHAPTER 5

Simple Science

This final chapter covers simple scientific concepts that young children can explore at an introductory level. They include action and reaction, absorption and evaporation, static and dynamic balance, wheels, gravity, flotation, sound, electricity, machinery, and magnetism.

Children can physically feel and see the concept of balance. They can hear sound. And they can see, to one extent or another, the remaining scientific concepts mentioned above. Of these concepts, only wheels can be experienced concretely. The rest are more abstract, but that doesn't mean children can't explore them. For example, children experience gravity every time they jump, hop, or leap into the air and come back down. They can understand that washing machines and dryers are both machines, and that many things, including various machines, use electricity. That doesn't mean they're ready to grasp how these things work. (Most of us adults don't even understand how such things as electricity *work!*)

Young children can, however, be introduced to these concepts (whether or not you name them) and can participate in physical experiences that will make these concepts more meaningful in their later school years.

Rock My World

Children intuitively understand that when they exert force on a certain object, they can send it into motion. This activity gives them an opportunity to observe this relationship. Although you will not be quoting Newton's third law of motion—for every action there is an equal and opposite reaction— that is exactly what the children will be experiencing.

To Have

No materials needed

To Do

- Have the children sit in pairs, with the soles of their feet together and their hands grasped in front of them.
- Encourage the children to rock back and forth. Point out that when one child leans back, the other must lean forward, and vice versa. Tell the children to move slowly and gently. How slowly can they go? When you feel the children can handle it responsibly, invite them to pick up the tempo.

More to Do

- If there is a seesaw on your playground, use it for another lesson on action and reaction. Further, seesaws are an introduction to the concepts of *levers* and *balance.*

Share the book *Scoop, Seesaw, and Raise: A Book About Levers* by Michael Dahl.

The Housepainter

This simple, fun activity allows children to witness absorption and evaporation simply by painting wood with water. In addition, the children get some upper-torso exercise!

To Have

Paintbrushes (1 per child)
Small buckets of water (1 per pair of children)

To Do

- Bring the children outside and tell them that they will pretend to be "housepainters." Show them how to dip their brushes into the bucket of water and "paint" the outside of the building, fence, or sidewalk.
- As the children paint, the wood, brick, or concrete will turn darker. Explain to the children that the water is going into tiny holes in the material and being *absorbed*.
- Take the children out a little while later to see how the material has changed. It should be lighter. Explain to the children that the water in the material has evaporated. The water that darkened the wall or fence turned into very tiny drops of water and went back up into the air. Explain that the water will help make clouds.

More to Do

- Invite the children to "paint" other things outdoors. Possibilities include paved areas, the jungle gym and slide, or the bark of a tree. Are there any differences in how these objects look after the children paint them? Does it take more water to darken some surfaces than other surfaces? Does the water disappear faster on some surfaces than on others?

Explores the concept of balance

Walking a Tightrope

Young children enjoy practicing their balancing skills, and if they have ever been to the circus, they will have double the fun with this activity! It provides practice with dynamic balance, which involves maintaining balance while moving.

To Have

Several long jump ropes

To Do

- Lay the jump ropes in straight lines on the floor.
- Challenge the children to take turns walking across them, pretending to be tightrope walkers at the circus. If necessary, remind them that tightrope walkers hold their arms out to the side to maintain their balance.

More to Do

- Once the children feel comfortable walking the tightrope in a forward direction, challenge them to try it moving sideways and, finally, backwards.

Mirette on the High Wire by Emily Arnold McCully is a Caldecott Award Winner that is a great accompaniment to this activity.

Play the song "High Wire Artist" by Hap Palmer, from the album titled *Easy Does It*. "Tiptoe on a Tightrope" is available on Brenda Colgate's *Silly Willy Moves Through the ABCs*.

Take an Air Walk

This simple activity helps children understand that air moves things. It also strengthens the children's powers of observation and provides an opportunity for them to get some exercise!

To Have

Large trash bag

To Do

- Go for a walk with the children on a breezy day. Challenge them to look for things that the air is moving. Some possibilities include flags, trees, leaves (both on and off the trees), clothes on a clothesline, flowers, and even litter.
- Tell the children that it is particularly important to keep the planet clean, and encourage them to collect any litter they see and put it in a trash bag.

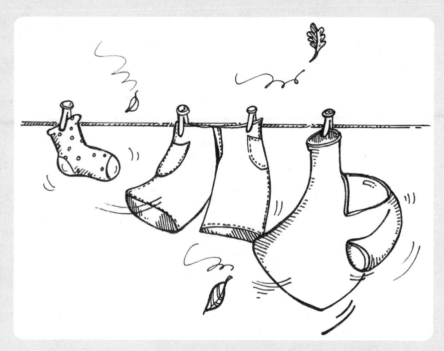

More to Do

- Expand this activity into a "light walk." Create awareness of light in the world around us by looking for interesting shadows created by buildings, trees, flagpoles, and so on.

Explores changing states of matter

I'm Melting!

When a substance melts, such as water or butter, it changes state from solid to liquid. Children can pretend they are the actual substances melting from one form to another. This activity is great for relaxation!

To Have

No materials needed

To Do

- Talk with the children about melting. Ask them if they can think of things that melt. Some examples might include a snowman in the sun, chocolate chips baking in a cookie, butter on a hot pancake, an ice cream cone on a hot day, and so on. See how many images the children can come up with.
- Next, have the children pretend that they are one of these things melting. Have them melt as slowly as they can. What happens when they get hotter? Can they melt more quickly?

More to Do

- If it is wintertime, bring the children outside to make a snowperson. Mark the date on the calendar. How many days or weeks does it take the snowperson to melt?

Share Raymond Briggs' *The Snowman* with the children.

The song "I Can Make a Snowman" is available on Carole Peterson's *H.U.M. All Year Long.*

'Round & 'Round

Through their toys, children are familiar with most, if not all, of the six simple machines: the lever, wheel, pulley, inclined plane, screw, and wedge. They just do not know the names for each. This activity explores one of these machines, the wheel, and helps to promote the children's problem-solving skills.

To Have
Parachute

To Do
- Have the children stand around the parachute, holding it at waist-height. Ask them to imagine the parachute is a wheel, and challenge them to make the wheel go around without moving from their places. How can they do it? (Answer: They rotate it by passing it either right or left.)
- Encourage the children to try turning their wheel at varying tempos, from very slow to very fast.

More to Do
- If the children can move from their places, how many different ways can they think of to make the parachute "wheel" go around? Possibilities include walking, tiptoeing, galloping, marching, and jumping in a circle while holding the parachute with one hand. Can the children find a way to make the parachute "wheel" go around while using both hands? (Answer: Facing the parachute and sliding to the side.) With all of these possibilities, encourage the children to make the wheel go in both directions.
- Take the children on a wheel walk. Look for wheels used in everyday life. Some examples include cars, bicycles, skateboards, grocery carts, wheelbarrows, and flagpole pulleys.

Share the book *What Do Wheels Do All Day?* by April Jones or *Big Wheels* by Anne Rockwell.

"The Wheels on the Bus" is available on Hap Palmer's *Early Childhood Classics* and on Bob McGrath's *Sing Along with Bob, Volume I.* "There's a Little Wheel" is a song that appears on Carole Peterson's *Stinky Cake.*

Introduces the concept of gravity

The Gravity of Gravity

Have the children ever heard the phrase "What goes up must come down"?
Why do they think this happens? Talk to the children about gravity. Explain
that gravity is something that pulls objects to Earth. Gravity is very
important. If we did not have gravity, we would go flying off into space!

To Have

Chiffon scarves (1 per child)

Lightweight balls (1 per child)

Beanbags (1 per child)

Parachute and cotton balls (optional)

To Do

- Have the children scattered throughout the activity area so they will not interfere with one another.
- Invite the children to toss their scarves into the air as "hard" as they can. Does the scarf come back down slow or fast? Does it make any difference how fast it comes down if they do not throw it hard?
- Next, have the children try the same experiment with a ball, and then a beanbag. Of these three items, which came down fastest? Which came down slowest? What makes each of these things come down? Why do some things come down faster than other things?

More to Do

- Consider conducting a similar experiment by having the children toss things into the air with the parachute. First, try cotton balls and then beanbags. Which is hardest to lift into the air? Which comes back down to the parachute the quickest?

The book *Gravity Is a Mystery* by Franklyn M. Branley is a perfect accompaniment to this activity. You may also want to read *What Is Gravity?* by Lisa Trumbauer.

Up, Up, & Away!

Young children are fascinated by things that float, so they will enjoy exploring this concept. They will especially enjoy imagining what it would be like if they could float in the air.

To Have

Bottle of bubbles
Feathers (1 per child, optional)
Parachute (optional)

To Do

- Explain to the children that some objects can float in the air similar to the way certain objects can float on water.
- Have the children blow bubbles and watch them float. Ask the children, "What kinds of things float? Are they light or heavy?"
- Invite the children to pretend that they are bubbles, floating gently through the air. Continue to blow bubbles to inspire the children as they pretend to float.

More to Do

- Take the children outside and blow bubbles for them to chase, catch, and pop!
- Give each child a feather, challenging each child to keep their feather afloat by blowing on it.

Share the book *Bubble Trouble* by Stephen Grensky.

The CD *Vincent and the Big Bad Kitchen Band* includes a song called "Double Bubble Bath."

Simple Science

Offers experience with flotation and gravity

What Goes Up

This activity is an exploration of air buoyancy and gravity. Although these are two fundamental principles of physics, the children are simply having a good time with balloons!

To Have

Inflated balloons (1 per child)

To Do

- Have the children toss their balloons into the air and watch them float. Can the children make the balloons go higher by throwing them harder? How else can they make the balloons go higher? How can the children keep the balloons in the air longer? (Because hand-eye coordination does not fully develop until age 9 or 10, the children may not yet be able to volley—strike in an upward direction—their balloons successfully.)
- Invite the children to catch their balloons as they float down to the ground. Have the children try to catch them at four different points: while the balloons are still high in the air, when they are at shoulder-height, when they are at the children's knees, and when they are almost touching the ground.

More to Do

- Give each pair of children an inflated balloon and challenge the pair to keep their balloon in the air for as long as they can. To make the activity more difficult, make it a rule that neither of the children can touch the balloon twice in a row (so they have to take turns tapping it).
- Encourage the children to practice volleying the balloon (keeping it in the air by striking or tapping it with their hands).
- Challenge the children to keep the balloon afloat with any body part other than their hands. Consider assigning specific body parts that the children can use. Possibilities include the elbows, head, knees, and feet.
- Challenge the children further by giving a group of three children two balloons to keep in the air.

Albert Lamorisse's *The Red Balloon* is a classic balloon story that makes a perfect accompaniment to this activity. Another book possibility is Jamie Lee Curtis' *Where Do Balloons Go?*

Music possibilities include Vincent's "Julia Noon's Balloon," from *Just One Step,* and "Blow the Balloon" from *Travelin' with Ella Jenkins.*

Sounds All Around

In this activity, children will explore ways to create a variety of sounds. It is a good opportunity to explain that sounds are created when things vibrate. While vibration is an important concept of physical science, this activity also covers the areas of literacy and music.

To Have

Paper

To Do

- Talk to the children about sound. What are some of the different sounds they hear every day?
- Ask the children to lightly place their fingertips under their chins and hum. Can they feel their throats *vibrating*? Now lead them in making loud vowel sounds: A-E-I-O-U. Do the vibrations feel different as they make different sounds?
- How else can the children use their bodies to make sounds? Possibilities include clapping hands, stamping feet, clucking the tongue, and shuffling feet. Challenge the children to make both loud and soft sounds. Explain that these sounds all involve vibrations.

More to Do

- Invite the children to move around the room, exploring possibilities for making different sounds. For example, knocking on the door will create a very different sound from crumpling a piece of paper.
- Pass around an 8½" by 11" sheet of paper, inviting each child to create a different sound with it. Possibilities include crumpling, tearing, flapping, blowing across it, and rubbing it between the palms.

Two excellent book possibilities are *Sounds All Around* by Wendy Pfeffer and *All About Sound* by Lisa Trumbauer.

A good choice for a musical accompaniment is "Sounds Around the World" from Hap Palmer's *Rhythms on Parade*.

Explores the concept of gravity

The Force

This fun activity gives children the opportunity to consider gravity, and to consider what it might be like to have zero gravity!

To Have

No materials needed

To Do

- To start, invite the children to stand in place and jump as high as they can into the air. Can they think of ways to go even higher? Have them try jumping in different ways such as hopping on one foot, making a long jump from one spot to another, or taking three steps and then leaping. Ask the children why they come back down to the ground every time.

- Talk to the children about astronauts. Explain how, in space, astronauts can float around weightlessly. Invite the children to pretend they are astronauts floating in space. Explain that they cannot experience zero gravity on Earth except in special machines that astronauts use for training. Nevertheless, they can still have fun pretending!

Read *Floating in Space* by Franklyn M. Branley.

A good piece to play while the children are pretending to float in space is "The Astronaut." This instrumental song can be found on the *Wiggle, Giggle, & Shake* CD by Rae Pica and Richard Gardzina.

Let It Flow!

When explaining electricity to young children, simply say that electricity is energy that flows through a wire. It goes from the wall plug through the lamp cord and into the light bulb, making it light up. This activity will help get that idea across, and it will introduce the concept of sequencing.

To Have

No materials needed

To Do

- Have the children stand side by side in a line, holding hands, with you at one end.
- Squeeze the hand of the child next to you. Explain that the squeeze represents electricity flowing from one place to another. Have the child next to you squeeze the hand of the next child, and so forth down the line. When the "electricity" reaches the last child, have that child say "Lights on!"
- Repeat this activity several times, letting the children take turns being the light at the end of the line.
- When the children are comfortable with this activity, challenge them to add an electrical sound effect "ZZZZT" and a little vibration to their bodies as they squeeze the hand of the next child.

More to Do

- Perform the above in a single-file line, with each child's hands on the shoulders of the child in front of her.

Read *What Is Electricity?* by Lisa Trumbauer.

The Wheels Go 'Round

Explain to the children that wheels can simply turn, or they can roll. Each action helps to do different kinds of work.

To Have

No materials needed

To Do

- Talk to the children about how wheels—like Ferris and steering wheels—turn. Then invite the children to show you how they can turn, first in one direction and then the other. Encourage them to try it at varying tempos and then at varying levels in space. For example, can the children turn while on tiptoe, on their knees, or on their bottom?
- Once they have had ample experience with turning, discuss the fact that wheels—like wheels on vehicles—also roll. Challenge them to pretend they are wheels rolling on the floor. (Allow the children to find their own ways of rolling.)

More to Do

- Play a game of Choo-Choo. Have the children form a single-file line, each with a hand on the shoulder of the child in front. The children's free arms move like wheels on a train as the line moves all around the area.
- Invite the children to stand in a close circle, with each child facing someone else's back. The children then extend their arms inside the circle so everyone's hands are touching, like spokes. Encourage them to go around and around, like a huge bicycle wheel turning.
- Play Bicycle Built for Two. Have the children pair off and lie on their backs with the soles of their feet together. Now encourage them to "pedal" while their feet continue to touch. Challenge the children to count the number of times they can pedal without breaking contact.
- Challenge the children to look for wheels while doing different kinds of work in the classroom or outdoors.

Read *Sophie's Wheels* by Debora Pearson.

Household Machines

Machinery fascinates children. This activity gives children a chance to pretend to be machinery, stimulating their imaginations along with their curiosity about how things work.

To Have

No materials needed

To Do

- Talk to the children about such household machines as a clothes dryers, washing machines, dishwashers, blenders, toasters, and can openers. What do these machines look like? How do they work? What parts do they have? How do those parts move?
- Invite the children to act out what it would look like to use each of these machines. (For example, the children might pretend to load or empty the washing machine or dryer.)
- Next, challenge the children to act out what it would look like to *be* each of these machines. Tell them they can be the whole machine, or they can be just one of its moving parts.

More to Do

- Have the children work together, pretending they are one big machine. Maybe they are machines that have never been invented before! Start by having one child perform a continuous movement in one spot, such as bending and straightening the knees. A second child joins in, standing near the first and contributing a different movement that relates in some way, without interfering, with the first. (For example, if the first child were bending and straightening the knees, the second child might move in opposition, straightening and bending the knees.) One after another, the children join in, each contributing a functioning part to the "machine." The machine can take on any shape, growing in different directions. Once the big machine is working together, encourage each "part" to make a different sound.

Read *Simple Machines* by Allan Fowler or *Household Inventions* by Natalie Lunis.

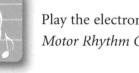

Play the electronic-sounding piece called "Move Like a Machine" from *Perceptual-Motor Rhythm Games* by Jack Capon and Rosemary Hallum.

Introduces the concepts of pitch and sound

Here's the Pitch

Sound is both a scientific and a musical concept. In this activity, children will explore pitch, which refers to the highness or lowness of a sound.

To Have

Water glasses (3 per child)

Pencils (1 per child)

Slide whistle (optional)

To Do

- Fill each child's three glasses with different amounts of water.
- Invite the children to use a pencil to tap lightly on each of their three glasses. Does each glass sound different? Which has the lowest sound? Which has the highest sound?
- Encourage the children to pour a little bit of water from one glass to another. Does it change the way each glass sounds?
- Finally, invite the children to make a little song by continuously tapping their glasses.

More to Do

- Invite the children to crouch low to the floor. Hum or use a slide whistle, gradually make a higher and higher sound. Encourage the children to rise up as the notes rise. As the notes lower, the children lower to the ground. Now, invite the children to make these sounds along with you as they move up and down.

Play "High & Low" from Rae Pica's *Moving & Learning Series: Preschoolers & Kindergartners* and "Scales" from Hap Palmer's *The Feel of Music.*

Simple Machines

As discussed in an earlier activity, the six simple machines are the lever, wheel, pulley, inclined plane, screw, and wedge. In this activity, children get to be wheels and levers at work as they pretend to be wheelbarrows.

To Have

Pictures of wheelbarrows

To Do

- Show the pictures of wheelbarrows to the children and discuss the work that wheelbarrows do.
- Divide the children into groups so that there is one adult for each group. Have the children form a single-file line. One at a time, each child becomes a "wheelbarrow" that the adult "gardener" pushes around the garden. The child places her hands on the floor and the adult lifts the child's feet into the air at an angle. The "gardener" wheels the child around by having her walk on her hands.

More to Do

- When the children are ready for the responsibility, have them work in pairs as wheelbarrow and gardener.
- Challenge the children to demonstrate the shapes of inclines and wedges with their bodies or body parts.
- If large, foam, inclined planes are available, give the children a chance to do log rolls down them.
- Invite the children to twist like screwdrivers and cut like scissors. Explain that these are simple machines called *levers*.

Michael Dahl has created a series of books about the exploration of simple machines. They include *Pull, Lift, and Lower: A Book About Pulleys*; *Twist, Dig, and Drill: A Book About Screws*; *Cut, Chop, and Stop: A Book About Wedges*; and *Tires, Spokes, and Sprockets: A Book About Wheels and Axles*.

Explores the concept of static balance

Buddy Balance

Balancing in a stationary position, like standing on one foot, is known as static balance. *This type of balance is typically more difficult for preschoolers than* dynamic balance, *which involves maintaining balance while moving. In this activity, children will help each other so that static balance is a little easier.*

To Have

No materials needed

To Do

- Have the children stand in a circle with their hands on the shoulders of the children on either side of them. Challenge them to rise onto tiptoe and to see how still they can hold themselves. Does it help if they hold their breath? What happens if they close their eyes?
- Once the children are familiar with the activity, try it again, counting the number of seconds the children can hold still. Repeat the activity a few more times, encouraging the children to increase the number of seconds they can balance.

More to Do

- Increase the challenge by asking each child to rise onto her tiptoes on just one foot. Can they all lean toward the center of the circle? Backwards? Can they each extend one leg into the center of the circle?
- Counterbalances involve partners creating balances that would not be possible for one person alone. Preschoolers will not be able to discover counterbalances on their own, but you can show them some possibilities and have them imitate them. Two of the simplest counterbalances involve partners leaning against each other, back to back, and partners facing each other, holding both hands and leaning away from each other.

Play the song "The Buddy Balance" on Brenda Colgate's *Silly Willy Moves Through the ABCs.*

Finding a Balance

This activity and its extensions will give children plenty of opportunity to experiment with static balance.

To Have

No materials needed

To Do

- Challenge the children to balance by holding as still as possible on the following body parts while you count to five:
  - Hands and knees
  - Hands and feet
  - Knees and elbows
  - Feet and bottom
  - Hands and bottom
- When you think they are ready, ask the children to balance on their bottom, knees, or tiptoes only. The ultimate challenge is to stand first on one foot and eventually on one foot on tiptoe!

More to Do

- The concept of balance and recovery involves nearly losing balance but then returning to the original position. Explore this concept with the children by asking them to balance on their knees or bottom only, and then leaning in different directions, going as far as they can without tipping over, and then straightening back up.

Share the book *Why Does It Fall Over? Projects About Balance* by Jim Pipe.

For a great musical balance activity, try "Tightrope" on *Steel Band Jamboree* by Frank Leto.

Promotes awareness of the concepts of balance and action and reaction

Tug-of-War

This age-old game will help children experience both balance and the concept of action and reaction. Because the children will use the force of their own bodies, this game also promotes muscular strength and muscular endurance, two health-related fitness factors.

To Have

Long jump rope made of natural fibers
2 short jump ropes
Scarf

To Do

- Outside, put the two short jump ropes parallel to each other, about 5' apart. These represent the goal lines for each team. Tie the scarf around the center of the long rope and hold it directly above the middle of the space between the two short ropes.
- Divide the children into two equal teams. Try to keep size and weight in mind, so that the teams are balanced. Have the teams form a single-file line with half on one side and half on the other side of the scarf.
- When the rope is taut, let go of the scarf. At your signal, the children pull on their end of the rope. The goal is for one of the teams to pull the scarf over their own goal line.

Read *Tug-of-War: All About Balance* by Kristen Hall.

To help develop balance, play Hap Palmer's "Tug-A-Tug" on *Can a Jumbo Jet Sing the Alphabet?*

A Magnetic Force

Magnets fascinate young children. While children may not be ready for an explanation of the north and south poles, they can pretend to be magnets attracted to metal.

To Have

Set of magnets (preferably straight)
Variety of items, both with and without iron in them

To Do

- To demonstrate that magnets only attract metal, hold a magnet near various pre-selected items. Engage the children in a discussion about why the magnet attracts certain objects but not others. Talk with the children about the kinds of things that have metal in them.
- Invite the children to move around the room pretending to be magnets. Ask them to touch all the different things in the room to which they think magnets might stick.

More to Do

- Demonstrate how magnets *attract* and *repel* each other, depending which sides face each other. Explain that magnets have two poles, one end is the "north pole" and the other end is the "south pole." Have the children show you what it would be like if two people were the north and south poles of two magnets. Ask the children if they have ever heard the phrase "opposites attract."
- Separate the children into two groups. Designate half of the children as north poles. Ask them to display what kinds of poles they are by each pointing a finger toward the ceiling. Designate the other half of the children as south poles, and ask them to indicate what kinds of poles they are by each pointing a finger toward the floor. Have the children begin to move about the room. At your signal, each child stops and looks toward the child closest to her. If the pairs represent opposite poles, they should "attract" by getting closer together. If they represent identical poles, they should "repel" by moving away from each other. After a short while, signal for the magnets to begin the process again.

Read *Magnets* by Anne Schreiber, or *What Magnets Can Do* by Allan Fowler.

Play the song "Magnets" from Maryann Harman's *Music Makes It Memorable.*

Simple Science 119

Glossary

Absorption: The process by which a solid or liquid substance takes up another solid or liquid substance (as when water is absorbed into wood or paper).

Air resistance: Refers to the fact that air has weight and that moving air pushes things.

Classifying: One of the five basic science-process skills, this refers to the sorting of objects according to such properties as color, size, shape, use, weight, and so forth.

Communicating: A basic science-process skill involving the communication of ideas and information, either in written or oral form.

Comparing: One of the basic science-process skills, related to the exploration of the differences and similarities of objects.

Dynamic balance: Refers to the process of maintaining balance while moving.

Earth and space science: Investigation of the properties of objects found on the earth and in space.

Evaporation: The process by which liquid becomes vapor.

Gravity: Earth's force of attraction upon objects at or near its surface.

Health science: Exploration of the human body and ways to stay healthy.

Hibernation: An inactive state resembling deep sleep in which some animals pass the cold winters.

Life science: The study of plants, animals, and ecology.

Measuring: The basic science-process skill related to quantitative observations about objects.

Metamorphosis: A change in the form and habits of an animal or insect during its development after birth or during hatching.

Observing: The basic science-process skill related to the gathering of information through the senses.

Physical science: The exploration of the properties of objects and materials.

Pitch: Refers to the lowness or highness of a sound.

Simple machines: The six simple machines are the lever, wheel, pulley, inclined plane, screw, and wedge.

Static balance: Balances that occur in a stationary position.

References

Charlesworth, R., & Lind, K.K. (2003). *Math and science for young children.* Clifton Park, NY: Delmar Learning.

Fauth, B. (1990). Linking the visual arts with drama, movement, and dance for the young child. In W.J. Stinson, (ed), *Moving and learning for the young child* (pp. 159-187). Reston, VA: American Alliance for Health, Physical Education, Recreation, and Dance.

Gardner, H. (1993). *Frames of mind: The theory of multiple intelligences.* New York: Basic Books.

Gilbert, A.G. (1977). *Teaching the three Rs through movement experiences.* Minneapolis, MN: Burgess.

Hannaford, C. (2005). *Smart moves: Why learning isn't all in your head.* Salt Lake City: Great River Books.

Jaques-Dalcroze, E. (1931). *Eurhythmics, art, and education* (F. Rothwell, Trans.; C. Cox, Ed.). New York: A. S. Barnes.

Jensen, E. (2000). *Brain-based learning.* San Diego: The Brain Store.

Jensen, E. (2001). *Arts with the brain in mind.* Alexandria, VA: Association for Supervision and Curriculum Development.

Index of Children's Books

Indexes

Index of Science Concepts & Skills

Index